ABRAHAM LINCOLN

ABRAHAM LINCOLN

Thomas Bracken

Introduction by James Scott Brady,
Trustee, the Center to Prevent Handgun Violence
Vice Chairman, the Brain Injury Foundation

Chelsea House Publishers
Philadelphia

CHELSEA HOUSE PUBLISHERS

EDITOR IN CHIEF Stephen Reginald
PRODUCTION MANAGER Pamela Loos
MANAGING EDITOR James D. Gallagher
PICTURE EDITOR Judy L. Hasday
ART DIRECTOR Sara Davis
SENIOR PRODUCTION EDITOR Lisa Chippendale

Staff for **Abraham Lincoln**
SENIOR EDITOR James D. Gallagher
ASSOCIATE ART DIRECTOR Takeshi Takahashi
DESIGNER Brian Wible
PICTURE RESEARCHER Patricia Burns
COVER ILLUSTRATION Michael Deas

First Printing

1 3 5 7 9 8 6 4 2

Library of Congress Cataloging-in-Publication Data

Bracken, Thomas.
Abraham Lincoln / Thomas Bracken.
p. cm.—(Overcoming Adversity)
Includes bibliographical references and index.
Summary: Presents the sixteenth president of the United States as
faced with both personal tribulations and national problems.
ISBN 0-7910-4704-0 (hc)   ISBN 0-7910-4705-9 (pb)
1. Lincoln, Abraham, 1809-1865—Juvenile literature.
2. Presidents—United States—Biography—Juvenile literature.
[1. Lincoln, Abraham, 1809-1865. 2. Presidents.] I. Title.
II. Series.
E457.905.B68   1998
973.7'092—dc21
[B]
                                                    97-48305

                                                         CIP
                                                          AC

CONTENTS

On Facing Adversity *James Scott Brady*   7

1   IN THE GARDEN OF GETHSEMANE   11

2   A HUMBLE BEGINNING   23

3   BUILDING A POLITICAL CAREER   35

4   HONEST ABE, THE RAIL SPLITTER   45

5   THE DARKEST HOUR   57

6   1863   75

7   "WE WILL GO BACK TO ILLINOIS"   87

Appendix A: Mary Todd Lincoln's Mental Problems   100

Appendix B: The Plot to Assassinate Lincoln   102

Appendix C: Civil War Associations   105

Chronology   106

Further Reading   108

Index   109

OVERCOMING ADVERSITY

TIM ALLEN
comedian/performer

JIM CARREY
comedian/performer

BILL CLINTON
U.S. President

JAMES EARL JONES
actor

ABRAHAM LINCOLN
U.S. President

WILLIAM PENN
Pennsylvania's founder

ROSEANNE
entertainer

ON FACING ADVERSITY

James Scott Brady

I GUESS IT'S a long way from a Centralia, Illinois, train yard to the George Washington University Hospital Trauma Unit. My dad was a yardmaster for the old Chicago, Burlington & Quincy Railroad. As a child, I used to get to sit in the engineer's lap and imagine what it was like to drive that train. I guess I always have liked being in the "driver's seat."

Years later, however, my interest turned from driving trains to driving campaigns. In 1979, former Texas governor John Connally hired me as a press secretary in his campaign for the American presidency. We lost the Republican primary to a former Hollywood star named Ronald Reagan. But I managed to jump over to the Reagan campaign. When Reagan was elected in 1980, I was "sitting in the catbird seat," as humorist James Thurber would say—poised to be named presidential press secretary. I held that title throughout the eight years of the Reagan administration. But not without one terrible, extended interruption.

It happened barely two months after the Reagan administration took office. I never even heard the shots. On March 30, 1981, my life went blank in an instant. In an attempt to assassinate President Reagan, John Hinckley Jr. armed himself with a "Saturday Night Special"—a low quality, $29 pistol—and shot wildly as our presidential entourage exited a Washington hotel. One of the exploding bullets struck me just above the left eye. It shattered into a couple dozen fragments, some of which penetrated my skull and entered my brain.

The next few months of my life were a nightmare of repeated surgery, broken contact with the outside world, and a variety of medical complications. More than once, I was very close to death.

The next few years were filled with frustrating struggles to function with a paralyzed right side, struggles to speak and communicate.

To people who face and defeat daunting obstacles, "ambition" is not becoming wealthy or famous or winning elections or awards. Words like "ambition" and "achievement" and "success" take on very different meanings. The objective is just to live, to wake up every morning. The goals are not lofty; they are very ordinary.

My own heroes are ordinary folks—but they accomplish extraordinary things because they try. My greatest hero is my wife, Sarah. She's accomplished a lot of things in life, but two stand out. The first has been the way she has cared for me and our son since I was shot. A tremendous tragedy and burden was dropped unexpectedly into her life, totally beyond her control and without justification. She could have given up; instead, she focused her energies on preserving our family and returning our lives to normal as much as possible. Week by week, month by month, year by year, she has not reached for the miraculous, just for the normal. Yet in focusing on the normal, she has helped accomplish the miraculous.

Her other most remarkable accomplishment, to me, has been spearheading the effort to keep guns out of the hands of criminals and children in America. Opponents call her a "gun grabber"; I call her a national hero. And I am not alone.

After a seven-year battle, during which Sarah and I worked tirelessly to educate the public about the need for stronger gun laws, the Brady Bill became law in 1993. It was a victory, achieved in the face of tremendous opposition, that now benefits all Americans. Since the law has been in effect, background checks have stopped 173,000 criminals and other high-risk purchasers from buying handguns, and the law has helped to reduce illegal gun trafficking.

Sarah was not pursuing fame, or even recognition. She simply started at one point—when our son, Scott, found a loaded handgun on the seat of a pickup truck and, thinking it was a toy, pointed it at Sarah. Fortunately, no one was hurt. But seeing a gun nearly bring a second tragedy upon our family, Sarah became determined to do whatever she could to prevent senseless death and injury from guns.

Some people think of Sarah as a powerful political force. To me, she's the person who so many times fed me and helped me dress during my long years of recovery.

Overcoming obstacles is part of life, not just for people who are challenged by disabilities, illnesses, or tragedies, but for all people. No matter what the obstacle—fear, disability, prejudice, grief, or a difficulty that isn't likely to "just go away"—we can all work to make this world a better place.

Abraham Lincoln reflects on the condition of the United States in this 1861 Matthew Brady photograph. At the time of his inauguration in March of that year, eight Southern states had announced they would leave the United States, and civil war appeared imminent.

1

IN THE GARDEN OF GETHSEMANE

THE SKY WAS OVERCAST, and a cold drizzle had turned into a light snow. It was the morning of February 11, 1861, and Abraham Lincoln, recently elected the 16th president of the United States, was about to embark on the long train ride from his hometown of Springfield, Illinois, to the nation's capital, Washington, D.C.

However, the words that Lincoln chose to address the crowd that had come to see him off that morning, one day before his 52nd birthday, did not reflect joy or happiness at taking the nation's highest office, but rather the pain and sorrow that he felt at that particular moment. To his well-wishers that morning, Lincoln confided:

> No one not in my situation can appreciate my feeling of sadness at this parting. To this place, and the kindness of these people, I owe everything. Here I have lived a quarter of a century, and have passed from a young to an old man. Here my children have been born, and one is buried. I now leave, not knowing when or whether ever I may return, with a task before me greater than that which rested upon Washington. Without the assistance of that Divine Being who ever attended him, I cannot succeed.

11

Lincoln did not underestimate the enormity of the task before him. America in 1861 was a divided nation and was on the verge of waging a civil war.

The primary issue that had torn the nation apart was slavery, which was vital to the economy of the southern half of the United States. In the early years of the 19th century, as the northern states started to become more industrialized, the South had remained primarily agricultural, and by mid-century its economy centered upon the growth of cotton. With the invention of the cotton gin by Eli Whitney in 1793, the cotton crop had become so profitable that soon the people of the South referred to it as "King Cotton."

However, raising cotton presented certain unique problems. Cotton could not be planted on the same field year after year, because the plant drained the soil of nutrients. Therefore, to raise a profitable crop, hundreds of acres of land had to be devoted to cotton fields. In these large plantations, some fields could be left fallow for a season to rejuvenate the soil. Another problem was that growing cotton was labor intensive. Many people were required to plant, tend, and pick the cotton. This was a long process, as tedious as it was difficult, and a large and submissive work force was required to make a profit. Southern plantation owners found a solution to their labor problems by using slaves.

Slavery had been introduced in America as early as 1619. By Lincoln's election in 1860, there were approximately four million African Americans living in bondage throughout the South. The plantation owners who profited from this system were determined to keep their slaves; this became increasingly difficult as opposition to the slave trade grew in the North. To offset this mounting criticism of their economic system, politicians from the South attempted to link the expansion of the American nation itself to the spread of slavery—as America expanded westward to achieve its self-proclaimed "Manifest Destiny," so

too would the institution of slavery. For each "free" state admitted to the Union, a "slave" state would also be added. As the nation grew, slavery would continue in half of the states.

On the other hand, citizens who opposed slavery, called abolitionists, started to demand that the slave trade be ended in the United States. Most of the abolitionists lived in the North.

In the South during the 18th and 19th centuries, cotton was king and African-American slaves were used as inexpensive labor on the large cotton plantations.

The political problems posed by the differences between the North and the South were first averted by the Missouri Compromise of 1820, which admitted Maine as a free state and Missouri as a slave state and prohibited slavery in the North. The Compromise of 1850 admitted California as a free state, allowed the people of Utah and New Mexico to decide by popular vote whether or not their states should allow slavery, and prohibited the slave trade in the District of Columbia. Throughout the 1850s, however, hostilities between the North and the South continually escalated. As Northern demands for the immediate abolition of slavery became more and more incessant, Southern determination to preserve its existence grew more and more pronounced.

The ill will between the North and the South was so explosive that from 1854 to 1856, when residents of the newly established territories of Kansas and Nebraska were allowed to settle the issue of slavery by popular vote, sympathizers of both proslavery and abolitionist causes resorted to violence, hoping their views would prevail. More than 200 people died as a result of this territorial civil war. The violence of "Bleeding Kansas" and other events propelled the nation closer and closer to an armed conflict, while offering little hope for negotiation or compromise.

In 1857, Northerners were outraged when the U.S. Supreme Court ruled against Dred Scott, an African-American slave who was seeking his freedom. The court's controversial decision was that all people born into slavery would be considered the property of their owners and that the U.S. Constitution prohibited Negroes from becoming citizens. After this decision, the most ardent opponents of slavery promised to actively assist slaves in their attempts to flee the plantations of the South.

Likewise, many Southerners became upset about John Brown's ill-fated raid on the federal arsenal at Harper's Ferry, Virginia, two years later. Brown was a well-known abolitionist who had used violence to free slaves in the past, and his raid on Harper's Ferry (October 16-18, 1859) was essentially an attempt to stir up slave revolts in the South. Although federal troops retook the fort from Brown's small rebel force and Brown himself was tried, convicted, and hanged for the attack, the raid convinced people throughout the South that Northerners were out to destroy their way of life.

Slavery was an issue that dominated the presidential election of 1860. Having secured the nomination of the recently formed Republican party at its Chicago convention, Lincoln repeatedly voiced his opposition to the extension of slavery in the western territories. He also echoed his party's broad support for higher tariffs, which, while highly favorable for Northern manufacturers, would be of little or no assistance to Southern farmers. (A tariff is a tax on imported goods which has the effect of making merchandise produced within this country cheaper to American consumers.)

His main opponent in the election that year was U.S. Senator Stephen Douglas of Illinois, with whom Lincoln had staged a memorable series of political debates two years earlier during an unsuccessful bid for the Senate. During the campaign, Douglas, a Democrat, had repeated his simple, politically evasive stance that slavery could only exist where it enjoyed local support. Although Lincoln had repeatedly insisted throughout the campaign that his only difference with his opponent lay in Douglas's professed neutrality to the moral implications of slavery, this did little to soften the fear with which most Southerners regarded him. The possibility of a Lincoln victory was perceived by the South as almost a direct invitation to war.

Lincoln's triumph in the polls can be viewed as a minor miracle. He presented an easy target of criticism to those who disagreed with him. In the judgement of many, he was a crude and unrefined "third-rate country lawyer" who could not escape his humble beginnings. He did not speak with good grammar, and he was a social misfit who con-

In 1857 the U.S. Supreme Court ruled that Dred Scott, and anyone else born into slavery, should be considered the property of his owner. Scott had argued that he should be freed because his owner had moved from a Southern slave state to a state where slavery was prohibited, then back to the South. The court ruling angered northern abolitionists.

In this painting, The Last
Moments of John Brown *by
Thomas Hovenden, abolitionist John Brown, who led an
ill-fated insurrection at Harper's Ferry in 1858, kisses a
small black child before being
hanged. Brown's raid, intended to encourage slaves to
rebel against their masters,
was quickly crushed by federal troops; nevertheless, the
people of the South believed
that all Northerners shared
Brown's views and wanted to
destroy their way of life.*

stantly resorted to telling coarse and clumsy jokes. A prod-
uct of America's uncivilized western frontier, Lincoln possessed only about one full year of formal education, and he
seemed most comfortable when in the company of his fellow backwoodsmen. Often clad in homely and well-worn
clothes, he walked with a slow and shuffling gait, which
lent to him an undignified air of casual constraint. His
brooding, even melancholy eyes were supported by a
peculiarly long neck. The unassuming six-foot-four-inch
Lincoln was once described by someone who knew him
well as "the ungodliest figure I ever saw." This does not
appear to be an inaccurate representation.

Many Americans viewed Lincoln as an unacceptable
candidate for the office of president, and his 1860 victory
in the polls was by no means a political landslide. He
received less than 40 percent of the popular vote, and his
winning margin over his closest rival, Douglas, was by
less than a half million votes. Of the four major candidates

(John C. Breckinridge and John Bell also ran, and between them they collected about 1.4 million votes), only Douglas had electoral votes from both slave and free states, and Lincoln failed to receive a single electoral vote in 15 different states. However, reflecting the deep division in the country that year, Lincoln did carry all 18 free states by a rather wide margin. He received 180 electoral votes to 72 for Breckinridge, 39 for Bell, and 12 for Douglas. This was the first time in the history of the United States that the North had used its numerical superiority to vote down the South in a national election.

Not surprisingly, there was widespread speculation that Lincoln's victory, rather than saving the country, would lead it to war. Signs of deepening Southern resentment toward him appeared the very day after his election, when news of it was carried under the heading "Foreign News" by the *Charleston Mercury* of South Carolina. The same day, the governor of that state officially advocated the purchase of arms and munitions by his state to enable it to wage an eventual war with its Northern neighbors. Three days later, South Carolina officials announced they would hold a state convention to consider the issue of secession (the process by which an individual state would withdraw from the Union), and within a month several other Southern states had also begun this process.

Talk quickly turned into reality. On December 20, 1860, South Carolina became the first state to secede from the Union. By the end of January, Florida, Mississippi, Alabama, Georgia, and Louisiana had joined her, with Texas soon to follow. These states formed the Confederate States of America, elected Jefferson Davis president, and seized federal forts and arsenals within their borders. At the start of a new year, citizens from both the North and the South were growing increasingly anxious—it was clear that the United States was no longer united, and war now seemed unavoidable.

Secession—and eventual war—was a situation that the

outgoing president of the United States, James Buchanan, had done little to prevent. As his term in the White House came to an end, President Buchanan told Congress that, although no state had the legal right to secede, the federal government had no legal power to forcibly prevent a state from leaving the union. Americans who were determined to preserve the Union at all costs, including Abraham Lincoln, viewed these words as almost a direct invitation to secede. Lincoln was so disheartened at Buchanan's failure to act that before his inauguration he confided to one of his associates:

> Every hour adds to the difficulties that I am called upon to meet, and the present administration does nothing to check the tendency toward dissolution. I, who have been called upon to meet this awful responsibility, am compelled to remain here, doing nothing to avert it or lessen its force when it comes to me. . . . I have read, upon my knees, the story of Gethsemane, where the son of God prayed in vain that the cup of bitterness might pass from him. I am in the garden of Gethsemane now, and my cup of bitterness is full and overflowing.

As Lincoln spoke to his neighbors during his final morning in Springfield, his words were greeted with a strange and awkward silence. A somber air hung heavily over the crowd. As the train puffed slowly out of the station, a few murmurs of farewell could be detected from the onlookers. Then isolated applause turned into a groundswell, and Lincoln's supporters at the station cheered and shouted. For one brief shining moment, the sadness had lifted from Lincoln's heart.

The train zigzagged across the nation on a roundabout route that would take 12 days and cover nearly 2,000 miles. In an attempt to get to know the people who had elected him, the soon-to-be president had decided to speak at public rallies in New York and Ohio and to address the state legislatures of these and three other states. Lincoln spoke so often on the journey that at times he even lost his

CHARLESTON

MERCURY

EXTRA:

Passed unanimously at 1.15 o'clock, P. M. December 20th, 1860.

AN ORDINANCE

To dissolve the Union between the State of South Carolina and other States united with her under the compact entitled " The Constitution of the United States of America."

We, the People of the State of South Carolina, in Convention assembled, do declare and ordain, and it is hereby declared and ordained,

That the Ordinance adopted by us in Convention, on the twenty-third day of May, in the year of our Lord one thousand seven hundred and eighty-eight, whereby the Constitution of the United States of America was ratified, and also, all Acts and parts of Acts of the General Assembly of this State, ratifying amendments of the said Constitution, are hereby repealed; and that the union now subsisting between South Carolina and other States, under the name of "The United States of America," is hereby dissolved.

THE

UNION

IS

DISSOLVED!

On December 20, 1860, South Carolina became the first state to attempt to secede from the United States of America when its lawmakers passed an ordinance to end its union with the other states. The Charleston Mercury, *the newspaper serving South Carolina's capital, trumpeted the news on the front page.*

A distant view of Lincoln's inauguration as the 16th president of the United States, on the afternoon of March 4, 1861.

voice, but everywhere he went the crowds that greeted him were friendly and enthusiastic. The sadness of Springfield seemed only temporary.

Troubling news, however, awaited him as he closed in on Washington. In Baltimore, Lincoln was informed that there was a plot to assassinate him, and he was forced to travel the rest of the way in a horse-drawn carriage. He arrived in the capital unannounced and incognito, shielded by the darkness of night. Ominously, these threats of assassination would continue to haunt him throughout his presidency.

Washington, D.C., was an uneasy and troubled city on

March 4, 1861, the day of Lincoln's inauguration. Infantry sharpshooters were stationed on the rooftops along Pennsylvania Avenue in an attempt to dissuade any would-be assassins. Companies of soldiers blocked off all cross streets leading to the Capitol. On Capitol Hill, where the president would take his oath of office, a battery of light artillery was vigilantly perched. The usual air of festivity marking these occasions was noticeably absent.

As he spoke, the new president chose his words carefully, aware of their far-reaching significance. Urging compromise rather than obstinacy and peace rather than war, Lincoln told his countrymen, "We [the North and the South] are not enemies, but friends. We must not be enemies. . . . The mystic chords of memory, stretching from every battlefield and patriot grave, to every living heart and hearthstone, all over this broad land, will yet swell the chorus of the Union, when again touched, as surely they will be, by the better angels of our nature."

But the "better angels" that Lincoln spoke of were never to appear. In 139 days, on a battlefield not far from the very ground on which he spoke that day, the first major engagement of the American Civil War would begin. For Abraham Lincoln and the nation that he led, the greatest challenge awaited.

Abraham Lincoln in 1846, after his move to Springfield, Illinois, and marriage to Mary Todd.

2

A HUMBLE
BEGINNING

UNLIKE MANY OTHER American presidents, men such as John F. Kennedy or Franklin D. Roosevelt, Abraham Lincoln was not born into wealth or privilege. His ancestors had moved from England to a small town in Massachusetts in 1637, and generation after generation of Lincolns were mostly small-time farmers who were constantly moving in search of land that would provide them with a decent living. Lincoln's grandfather had moved to Kentucky in the early 1780s, and it was in that state, on February 12, 1809, that Abraham Lincoln was born to Thomas and Nancy Hanks Lincoln. He was born in a log cabin and named for his grandfather, Abraham.

Winters in Kentucky are often quite cold, and Abraham's earliest memories were of trying to warm himself next to his mother on particularly bitter winter evenings. The Kentucky weather was the earliest challenge of Lincoln's life—years later he would recall walking to school in winter months with a warm potato to protect his fingers from the numbing chill. The Lincolns were so poor that they could not afford to buy gloves for their children.

Thomas Lincoln, Abraham's father (right), spent his life farming. After Abraham's mother Nancy died, Thomas married Sara Bush Johnston (left). She instilled in the young Lincoln an interest in books and education that was to remain with him all his life.

The young Abraham was not, however, a regular schoolgoer—in fact, the total of his formal education came to a little more than one year. His parents never really expected him to amount to much, and the only reason they sent him to the "A-B-C school" two miles from his home was to provide company for his sister, Sarah, who they apparently believed had a brighter future. This was not that unusual for young farm boys born on the western frontier, as often their services were required on the farm. Lincoln later described his early life as a time of backbreaking labor in which he performed chores that ranged from feeding the pigs and cows, chopping wood for the fire, or

heating corn into meal. The chores lasted from early morning to late in the evening, in all types of weather, and there
always seemed to be more time spent on work than on
play.

When Abraham was seven, his family moved to Indiana, and the years that followed were ones of desperate
loneliness for the young boy, made even worse by the
sudden death of his mother when he was only nine. Without Nancy Lincoln to keep the household functioning, the
Lincolns lived in near squalor.

Thomas Lincoln soon remarried, however, and Abraham's new stepmother, Sarah Bush Johnston, was able to

instill in the youth a thirst for books and the knowledge they contained. Among Abraham's favorites were *The Pilgrim's Progress*, *Robinson Crusoe*, and biographies of George Washington and Benjamin Franklin. By reading these and other books, the young, impressionable Lincoln was able to learn about patriotism and the power of endurance, conquest, and human weakness, all lessons that would remain with him throughout adulthood. In his persistent efforts to educate himself, he also read *Lessons in Elocution*, by William Scott, and William Grimshaw's *History of the United States*, which contains the line, "Let us not only declare by words, but demonstrate by our actions, that all men are created equal." He borrowed these books from neighbors all over the county. Lincoln also studied the Bible, probably the only book the family actually owned, and in his later writings he often used quotations from scripture.

Lincoln's later attitude toward slavery may have been influenced by his father's habit of hiring the teenaged Abraham out to work for other families while keeping the pay for himself (this was legal in Indiana at the time). As a result of this practice, Abraham distanced himself psychologically from his father during this period of his life. Their relationship was never close, and biographers of Lincoln claim that he blamed his father for not being able to provide him with the emotional support that he needed after his mother's death. Years later Abraham would admit that he further resented his father because he choose to live where "there was absolutely nothing to excite ambition for education."

Isolated events from these years allow a glimpse of the future president's character development. While still in his teens he wrote essays against cruelty to animals and drunkenness, and he once saved a drowning dog by jumping into an icy river. Another time he rescued a stranger who happened to be on the losing end of a wrestling match.

The tall and angular Lincoln was quite skilled in this sport, and as a young man he had developed a local reputation as a talented wrestler. In a series of informal matches, he had put together an impressive string of victory after victory, and local supporters claimed that he was the finest wrestler not only in the county, but quite possibly in the entire state.

His first defeat, then, was for Lincoln as harsh as it was unexpected, but he calmly dusted himself off, congratulated the victor, and immediately challenged him to a rematch, in which Lincoln prevailed. A determined Abraham then won the third and decisive match. Even as a young man, the word "quit" was clearly not in Lincoln's vocabulary.

Resentful of his father and tired of the hardships of farming, Lincoln agreed to pilot a flatboat down the Mississippi River when he turned 18, the earliest age that he could legally leave his father. The parting between father and son was to be final; they would never see each other again. Lincoln seemed particularly eager to leave.

His journey down the Mississippi began an unremarkable 10-year period in Lincoln's life where he would work, at various times, as a carpenter, a soldier in the Black Hawk War of 1832 (this was a brief conflict between Native Americans and Illinois settlers; Lincoln was not involved in any fighting), a merchant, a store clerk, a blacksmith, a riverboat pilot, a surveyor, a lawyer, and a politician. During this period he was, in his own words, "a piece of floating driftwood."

Though burdened by debt as the result of an unsuccessful stint as a retail grocer in New Salem, Illinois, Lincoln's love of learning caused him to gravitate towards a career in law and politics. Whether Lincoln was motivated by financial need (he remained plagued by debt for most of his life) or by a sincere desire to help those around him (he once remarked to a close friend, "How hard it is to die, and leave one's country no better than if one had never lived"), this decision was the first step on the long road that would eventually lead to his revered place in the history of his nation.

Lincoln, living in New Salem, Illinois, first campaigned for public office in 1832 when he ran for a seat in the Illinois state legislature. Although he won nearly all the votes in his own community, he lost the election because he was not well known through the county. Although this would not be the first campaign for political office that Lincoln would lose during his career, this 1832 race was the only election by popular vote that he ever lost.

A lack of ego seems to have safeguarded the young politician against the perils of ambition—an early campaign circular that Lincoln distributed to the voters announced, "I was born, and have ever remained, in the most humble walks of life. I have no wealthy or popular relatives or friends to recommend me. . . . If the good people in their wisdom shall see fit to keep me in the background, I have been too familiar with disappointment to be very much chagrined." By stressing dignity despite his poor beginnings, Lincoln was saying that poverty would never keep him down and that any man who owed all his advantages to himself possessed an unlimited future.

Lincoln was more successful in his second bid for the Illinois legislature, in 1834, and he was reelected in 1836, 1838, and 1840. Lincoln was a member of the newly formed Whig Party, created in 1834 to oppose President Andrew Jackson's policies. Prominent members of the Whig Party included Henry Clay and Daniel Webster, and the party's national political agenda, based on Alexander Hamilton's Federalist economic policy, included the institution of protective tariffs and continuation of a national bank. Both of these suggestions appealed to merchants and manufacturers.

In 1837, Lincoln moved to Springfield, Illinois, a small town of 1,500 people. Springfield had no sidewalks, hogs and livestock walked freely in the streets, and the smell of

manure was easily detectable throughout the town. Historical accounts reveal that the year Lincoln arrived, the town supported two clothing stores, one bookstore, six churches, two newspapers (one supported Democrat policies and the other Whig), 18 doctors, and 11 lawyers. The number of lawyers grew to 13 in April 1837, when Lincoln opened a law firm with an associate named John Stuart.

In 1833, Lincoln and a partner, William Berry, bought this general store in New Salem, Illinois; however, the venture was a financial failure and left Lincoln deeply in debt.

In 1837, Abraham Lincoln moved to Springfield, Illinois, a small town of about 1,500 residents, and opened a law practice. This woodcut of the period is a view of the town shortly after Lincoln's arrival.

Springfield at that time was similar to many of the other small towns that sprang up on the nation's western frontier. A bustling city, it had managed to escape the hard financial times that much of the country was suffering through as a result of the Panic of 1837, a banking crisis, and for its citizens it offered the promise of a prosperous future. This appealed to Lincoln, who was constantly challenged by limited resources.

The United States, particularly its northern regions, was in a state of constant change at that time, and the threat this posed to the existing social order did not escape Lincoln's scrutiny. He looked about him and saw outbreaks of mob violence from Maine to Louisiana, as well as a constant stream of immigration that was changing the makeup of the nation. Spurred on by the development of canals and railroads, the United States was in the throes of a transportation revolution, and with the country's boundaries stretching further and further west, the national sense of political unity was constantly being weakened. With the

abolitionist movement growing throughout the North, the
nation was regionalized like never before.

The cloud of uncertainty that hovered over the nation in
1840 helped Lincoln define his political philosophy. Lincoln believed the champion of law was the advocate of
virtue. This virtue could only be achieved by strict adher-
ence to the principals found in the United States Constitution, written in 1787. As Lincoln wrote:

> Let every American, every lover of liberty, every well
> wisher to his posterity, swear by the blood of the
> Revolution, never to violate in the least particular, the laws
> of the country; and never to tolerate their violation by
> others. . . . Let reverence for the laws, be breathed by every
> American mother, to the lisping babe, that prattles on her
> lap; let it be taught in schools, in seminaries, and in col-
> leges; let it be written in Primers, spelling books, and in
> Almanacs; let it be preached from the pulpit, proclaimed
> in legislative halls, and enforced in courts of justice. In
> short, let it become the political religion of the nation.

What Lincoln feared in 1840 and would continue to fear
for the rest of his days was the power of uncontrolled emo-
tions. It was this emotion, or as he defined it, "passion,"
that would, two decades later, spur Americans to takes
arms against their fellow Americans. In Lincoln's judgement, the only way to conquer this passion was by listen-
ing to reason, which meant obeying the laws of the land. It
is this philosophy which drove Lincoln in his determined
refusal to allow the South to secede from the United States
in the Civil War.

Affairs of the heart competed with Lincoln's legal
pursuits in his early years at Springfield. A half-hearted
marriage proposal that was eventually rejected by the lady
to whom it was offered once again stirred in Lincoln feelings of inferiority. After the ill-fated affair, the struggling
attorney concluded, "I have now come to the conclusion
never again to think of marrying; and for this reason, I can
never be satisfied with any one who would be blockhead

Mary Todd, a vivacious and cultured young woman, took Abraham Lincoln's heart when they met in Springfield in 1840. The couple were married in November 1842.

enough to have me." But Lincoln penned these words in 1837, and his determination to live out his life as a single man faded three years later when he met the sophisticated and cultured Mary Todd at a party hosted by one of Springfield's wealthiest families. He was immediately captivated by the 22-year-old daughter of a prosperous banker and merchant, and he soon began seeing her regularly. Lincoln became helplessly in love with her, unable to resist the young lady's combination of intelligence, beauty, and wit. Overcoming his fear of intimacy with women, Lincoln asked her to marry him, and they became engaged sometime around Christmas of 1840.

The engagement was not a smooth one, and perhaps sensing her family's deep misgivings, Mary severed it. For the young lovers, however, the parting was only a temporary one. On November 4, 1842, at a wedding ceremony presided over by an Episcopal minister, a nervous Abraham Lincoln placed on his wife's finger a ring engraved with the words "Love is eternal."

The next two years would be eventful for the newlyweds. On August 1, 1843, their first son, Robert Todd Lincoln, was born. The next year they bought a small two-story house for $1,200, the first house that Lincoln had ever owned.

The Lincoln family remained financially troubled. In 1841, Lincoln and Stuart had dissolved their practice, and Lincoln opened a new law firm in Springfield with Stephen Logan. Business was steady but not spectacular, and although the practice provided a full caseload, it did not produce full pockets for the partners. Forced to charge low fees for his services due to the many lawyers he was competing with, Lincoln's annual income from the partnership never exceeded $1,000. In 1844, with a wife and small child to feed and a mortgage to pay off, Lincoln dissolved this practice and entered into a partnership with William Herndon, with whom he would remain close friends for the rest of his life. Better days, he hoped, were on the horizon.

Around this time, Lincoln wrote to a friend, "I have done nothing to make any human being remember that I have lived. Yet what I wish to live for is to connect my name with the events of my day and generation, to link my name with something which will be of interest to his fellow man." Today, the letter seems almost a prophesy. The man who wrote it could not have been aware of the journey that awaited him.

Lincoln poses for a daguerreotype in Chicago, 1854.

3

BUILDING A
POLITICAL CAREER

THE NEXT FEW YEARS were busy ones for Lincoln and were the happiest period of his professional life. For his new bride, however, the adjustment to marriage was not at all smooth. Her husband's meager salary presented many hardships to the former Southern belle, who was accustomed to a life of comfort and leisure on a large mansion. Their small, confining quarters began to grate on her, more so in 1846 with the birth of the couple's second son, Edward Baker Lincoln. Besides the normal rigors of pregnancy, for the first time in her life she had to cook, sew, and clean mud off the floors of her tiny home. A daily quota of dirty diapers did little to cheer her.

Alarmingly, her health began to deteriorate. Mary began to suffer from painful headaches, which she casually attributed to allergies. The headaches made her grouchy and irritable, and at times she screamed at unsuspecting strangers for no reason at all. At one time she even attacked her husband by hurling pieces of firewood at him. Mary Lincoln also developed an irrational fear of lightning and became terrified at the mere sight of dogs. As her husband was often away for many nights at a time, traveling around the county to perform his duties as a lawyer, she was forced to face these problems alone, which further increased her insecurity.

Despite her illness, she remained an ardent supporter of her husband's efforts to establish a successful legal career. Lincoln devoted more and more of his energy to his law practice after stepping down from the state legislature in 1842, and he developed a reputation throughout Illinois as a skilled and talented lawyer. Traveling around the state on the law circuit, he sometimes spent more than three months at a time away from home. Friends of Lincoln would later claim that these months away from home would have an indelible impact on his political future; an intimate confidant of his later wrote:

> [H]e was constantly out with the common people, mingling with the politicians, discussing public questions with the farmers who thronged the offices in the Court House and the State House, and exchanging views with the loungers who surrounded the stove on winter evenings in the village store. The result of this continuous contact with the world was that he was more thoroughly known than any other man in the community.

Abraham and Mary missed each other greatly during these times apart, and when together they enjoyed each other's company immensely. Although they shared an interest in and affection for their children, the burden of raising them fell mostly on Mary. She seemed to take equal joy in the accomplishments of both her husband and her children—baby's first step was the same cause for celebration as a victory for Abraham in an important trial. The rare evenings that Lincoln found himself at home were spent in quiet reading, as the man with only one year of formal education was determined to learn as much about the world around him as possible. On the shelf next to his bed were volumes of Shakespeare, Byron, Ralph Waldo Emerson, and Walt Whitman. Lincoln was perhaps aware that the growing town of Springfield was not nearly

big enough to hold him there forever.

For two years, from 1847–49, it wasn't. During this time Lincoln served his only term in the U.S. Congress. For both Abraham and Mary, however, their stay in Washington was easily forgotten.

In 1847, the U.S. capital had 40,000 residents, of whom 8,000 were free blacks and 2,000 were slaves. It was by far the largest city that either one of them had ever known, and at first it offered a sense of adventure and intrigue. They frequently attended the theater and whenever possible were present at the biweekly concerts provided by the Marine Band, which they both found immensely entertaining. For intellectual stimulation, they sat in on lectures offered by local academics or visiting foreign dignitaries.

Abraham Lincoln stands outside the house he bought in Springfield in 1844, the only house he ever owned. With him is his son Willie.

But the strangeness of the city and its helter-skelter
pace eventually unnerved the normally placid Mary. It was
a noisy city, and construction seemed everywhere—not
only was the Capitol building not yet completed in 1847,
but the cornerstone to the Washington Monument had yet
to be laid. Her husband's demanding schedule left him little time to spend with his wife and family, and the city
which had previously seemed exotic now seemed strange,
and even a bit dangerous. With no friends in Washington,
D.C., she became dissatisfied with city life. Six months
after she arrived in the city, she took her children and
returned to the more friendly atmosphere of her father's
home in Kentucky. Lincoln was left alone.

For him, the time was equally as unnerving, but for different reasons. Until this time in his life, Lincoln had felt ambivalent toward slavery—although he was convinced that slavery was wrong and he was personally opposed to it, he was by no means an abolitionist. Lincoln's mixed feelings on the matter can best be revealed by a motion he sponsored before the Illinois state legislature in 1837, as well as a personal statement concerning it that he authored later. In the first, his ambivalence was plain to see:

> [I] believe that the institution of slavery is founded on both injustice and bad policy, but the promulgation of abolition doctrines tends rather to increase than abate its evils. . . . I believe that the Congress of the United States has no power under the Constitution to interfere with the institution of slavery in the different States.

In the second document, his personal opposition to slavery becomes obvious:

> There is no permanent class of hired laborers amongst us. Twenty-five years ago I was a hired laborer. The hired laborer of yesterday labors on his own account today, and will hire others to labor for him tomorrow. Advancement—improvement in conditions—is the order of things in a society of equals. As labor is the common burden of our [human] race, so the effort of some to shift their share of the burden onto the shoulders of others is the great durable curse of the race. Originally a cure for the transgression upon the whole race, when, as by slavery, it is concentrated on a part only, it becomes the double-refined curse of God upon his creatures.

Taken together, these statements clarify the contradictory feelings that Lincoln had on the subject of slavery. Although he was opposed to slavery on a moral basis, for both practical and philosophical reasons he could not favor its elimination in states where it already existed. Lincoln had a deep reverence for the principals of law in the U.S. Constitution, and as hard as he looked he simply could find no basis whatsoever, under the Constitution, for ordering the immediate end of slavery. The solution to the

Slave auction houses were common sights in Washington, D.C., when Lincoln was serving a term as a representative to Congress. During this period, Lincoln's opposition to slavery deepened, and he proposed legislation that would free slaves in the District of Columbia. However, the measure failed to pass in Congress.

problem, Lincoln felt, was to forbid its extension into territories where slavery did not already exist; this would then lead to its eventual death. This did not, however, lessen the moral distaste that he felt for the institution in any way.

Lincoln's attitudes concerning slavery were of course formulated in Illinois, a northern state. Before he moved to the capital, Lincoln had spent nearly his entire life in the North, with the exception of an occasional flatboat journey down the Mississippi River, and had never personally witnessed the human cruelty that slavery involves. But in

Washington, D.C., he could no longer isolate himself from these horrors. Just seven blocks from the Capitol building stood the warehouse of Franklin & Armfield, the country's largest slave trader, and during his stay in Washington, D.C., Lincoln often witnessed the live auction of human beings and the brutal treatment that was part of the lives of the 2,000 slaves who lived in the city. This caused him to realize that as long as these horrors were allowed to continue, the United States could never claim to be the "home of the free" or dedicated to the idea of liberty. This not only embarrassed the future president but it also offended him.

It is not surprising, then, that his only attempt at legislation as the sole Whig representative from Illinois was his introduction of a bill which proposed the gradual and compensated emancipation of slaves in the District of Columbia, which could only be accomplished with the consent of the "free white citizens" of the district. But there was little support for Lincoln's measure—by taking the middle ground, with its provision of compensation to the slaveholders, it displeased abolitionists, while slave holders were opposed to relinquishing their free labor at any cost. The bill died an anonymous death, without ever having been seriously considered.

Lincoln returned home a spiritually wounded man who was beginning to seriously question his party's political future. Previously he had been convinced that the Whig Party was established on moral principals which coincided with American life, but after two disheartening years in Washington, D.C., he wasn't so sure. In the words of Lincoln biographer David Herbert Donald, Lincoln had previously felt that:

> Economically it [the Whig Party] stood for growth, for development, for progress. [Henry] Clay's American System [a plan to unite America with a system of roads and canals] sought to link the manufacturing of the Northeast with the grain production of the West and the cotton and

tobacco crops of the South, so that the nation's economy would become one vast interdependent web. When economic interests worked well together, so would political interests, and sectional rivalries would be forgotten in a powerful American nationalism.

Lincoln's devotion to the principals once embodied by the Whigs was illustrated in a letter he wrote to a young man who wanted to study law with Lincoln as his mentor. In the letter, Lincoln speaks of the wonderful miracle of American life: that no matter how poor or what circumstance a person is born into, through hard work and determination, that person can succeed in all of life's endeavors. "If you are resolutely determined to make a lawyer of yourself, the thing is more than half done already," Lincoln wrote. "It is but a small matter if you read with anybody or not. I did not read with anyone. Get the books, and read and study them till you understand them in their principal features, and that is the main thing. It is of no consequence to be in a large town while you are reading. I read at New Salem, which never had three hundred people living in it. . . . Always bear in mind that your own resolution to succeed is more important than any one thing."

But by 1850, Lincoln could not ignore the disappointment he felt in his own political party. The issues that it had always stood for—a protective tariff, a national bank, federal support for internal improvements—all seemed as outdated as the men who led the party, such as Daniel Webster and Henry Clay.

By 1850, Americans seemed more concerned with growing their young nation and with personal gain than with equality of opportunity for all. This was shown by U.S. involvement in the Mexican War of 1846 and the stampede for gold after its discovery in California three years later. To Lincoln, the Whig political party, once dedicated to the advancement of the common people, now seemed hopelessly adrift and more concerned with its own legacy of military conquest. The Whig nomination of

Zachary Taylor, the leader of the American assault on Mexico, for the presidency of the United States in 1848 left a bitter taste in Lincoln's mouth, one which Taylor's subsequent victory in the polls did little to remove. That his party was never able to address the issue of slavery to his own satisfaction was another source of annoyance for Lincoln. It was one of his most frustrating political hours.

This photograph of Lincoln was taken in August 1860, as he was campaigning for the presidency of the United States.

4

HONEST ABE, THE RAIL SPLITTER

FOR ABRAHAM LINCOLN, the new decade began with sadness. On February 1, 1850, the Lincolns' four-year-old son Edward died of pulmonary tuberculosis after a difficult two-month struggle. Both parents were devastated by this cruel twist of fate, particularly Mary, who had recently lost her father and grandmother to illness. For Lincoln, the next few years continued to mix good fortune with tragedy. In December 1850 Mary delivered another boy, named William Wallace, and in 1853 the couple had another son, whom they named Thomas. Their choice of a name was not insignificant—Lincoln's father, also named Thomas, had died a few months before the birth, and Lincoln had been unable to attend the funeral. Perhaps naming his youngest son after his own father was Lincoln's way of easing some of the guilt he must have felt for missing the funeral. Because the infant Thomas was unusually small when he was born, the boy was nicknamed "Tad" (short for tadpole), and this nickname stuck with him for the rest of his life.

After Edward's death, Mary Todd Lincoln's behavior began to grow increasingly unpredictable, and Abraham directed more and more

Henry Clay (1777-1862), one of the leaders of the Whig party, was the primary creator of the Compromise of 1850, which temporarily defused the tension between North and South. In the long run, however, all the Compromise of 1850 did was delay the Civil War.

attention to his children. Though his law firm hinted, for the very first time, at the possibility of providing him with a more than adequate income, he remained active in political affairs. He continued to oppose the extension of slavery into new territories, and he endorsed the Compromise of 1850, which had developed into one of the great dramas of American politics.

When the U.S. Congress had met in December 1949, it was bitterly divided over slavery and other issues. Some political leaders feared the Southern states would secede because of the division, and a variety of proposals were drafted to prevent secession. Five of these proposals were passed jointly and came to be known as the Compromise of 1850.

Although when it was passed the compromise was

perceived as defusing many explosive national issues, it
merely served as a temporary halt to the rising animosities
that were tearing the nation apart. Its measures provided
both Northerners and Southerners with equal reason to
celebrate and grumble. Its admission of California into the
Union as a free state permanently ended the existing
balance of slave and free states, which represented a
significant triumph for the North. Southerners, however,
were consoled by a provision that called for a stricter
Fugitive Slave Act to retrieve runaways, as well as the fact
that, although the slave trade was to be abolished in the
District of Columbia, slavery itself would be allowed to
continue there. The remaining clauses of the Compromise
of 1850 dealt with the admission of two new territories,
Utah and New Mexico, but did not address the issue of
slavery in either territory.

Although Congress passed this legislation as a compromise, few Americans believed that it served as a final
solution to their country's domestic problems. All that the
Compromise of 1850 really accomplished was to
temporarily delay the almost inevitable war between the
North and the South.

After the passage of the Kansas-Nebraska Act in 1854,
Lincoln decided to speak out. He was personally opposed
to this legislation because it allowed settlers of the Kansas
and Nebraska territories to decide by popular vote whether
slavery would be allowed in each territory. This was called
"popular sovereignty." Lincoln felt that popular sovereignty
was a dangerous idea. He feared that opening up new areas
for possible expansion of slavery would create violent
competition between Northerners and Southerners to
settle the land. He was proven correct when the Kansas
territory became a battleground for abolitionist and
proslavery settlers. The conflicts in "Bleeding Kansas"
included rigged elections, lynch mobs, and rioting.

In October of 1855, Lincoln delivered one of the most
memorable speeches of his political career. In the hall of

The Kansas-Nebraska Act, passed in 1854, permitted settlers in the Kansas and Nebraska territories to decide by popular vote whether slavery would be allowed in each territory. This act led to violence between pro-slavery and abolitionist groups who tried to settle the land. This group of Free-Soilers, so named because they opposed the extension of slavery into new territories, stands ready to defend Lawrence, Kansas, against a group of pro-slavery Missourians in November 1855.

the Illinois House of Representatives, wearing neither jacket nor tie, he spoke with a voice that was clear and sharp on that hot and stuffy afternoon.

In his speech, Lincoln for the very first time expressed his opposition to slavery on a moral basis. It would be this thinking which would define him as one of America's greatest and most enlightened political leaders. He claimed that the licensing or exclusion of slavery in new U.S. territories hinged solely on the question of "whether a Negro is not or is a man." In Lincoln's estimation, the answer to this was clearly affirmative, and he cited the immortal words of Thomas Jefferson in the Declaration of Independence that all men, even those not endowed with outstanding talents and abilities, are created equal. Consequently, Lincoln reasoned, there was absolutely no moral basis for slavery, as the black man in America was, above all else, a man. Lincoln told his listeners: "No man is good enough to govern another man, without that other man's consent. I say this is the leading principle—the sheer anchor of American Republicanism."

This was a bold message which clearly conveyed the moral contempt Lincoln felt for slavery. Lincoln by now had reached a highly passionate state and, speaking with soaring eloquence, he roared to the crowd, "There can be no moral right in connection with one man's making a slave of another." One person who witnessed the speech later remarked that when Lincoln spoke these words he "quivered with feeling and emotion," and "his feelings once or twice swelled within."

Many who attended the speech cheered this message, and some even waved their handkerchiefs as a show of support. But more importantly, that same week some of the more prominent antislavery advocates in the region announced their intentions of organizing a Republican party in Illinois, based in large part on the sentiments of Lincoln's speech.

The new Republican Party was a loose coalition of varied political interests. These included abolitionist Whigs, discontented Democrats known as "Free Soilers" who opposed the extension of slavery, and the antislavery elements of the Native American Party, which had been formed to limit immigration into the United States. By calling themselves Republicans, the new political party invoked the memory of Thomas Jefferson, a man dedicated to the principles of equality and democratic government.

For several years Lincoln had been disgruntled with the Whig Party, so the new Republican Party appealed to him. He had been disappointed in 1854 when his effort to win a U.S. Senate seat from Illinois failed, and he blamed his defeat on the political backstabbing of his own party. The victory of Lyman Trumball that year was achieved at the state convention only after much back-room bargaining, and this caused Lincoln to feel personally betrayed by his own party. (It was not until 1913, with the passage of the 17th Amendment, that representation in the Senate was

In 1858, Lincoln and Senator Stephen Douglas staged a memorable series of public debates while campaigning for election to the Senate. Seven debates were held, with the future of slavery one of the more important issues discussed. Although Lincoln lost the Senate election, the debates had drawn national attention, making him a household name before the 1860 presidential election.

determined by popular vote. Until then, it had been determined at state conventions such as this, which often resulted in selections of dubious integrity.) Lincoln decided to make a final break from the Whig party.

Uncertainty surrounded the first Republican National Convention, held in 1856 in Philadelphia. Although there was some speculation that Supreme Court Justice John McLean would secure the nomination as the Republican candidate for president of the United States, the strongest candidates appeared to be either William Seward of New York or Salmon P. Chase of Ohio. However, the Republicans nominated John C. Frémont, a popular soldier and former senator who was nicknamed the "Pathfinder of the West" because of his explorations of the Rocky Mountains, and sentiment began to build to name Lincoln as his running mate. Although this spot on the ticket was eventually secured by William Dayton, a former senator from New Jersey, Lincoln was pleased after the convention. His political star was rising, and he had even begun to secure a national reputation for himself. This seemed unlikely to the man born in a log cabin with no formal education, often penniless and despondent in his personal life. It was, however, the reward for his refusal to surrender to the challenges and setbacks offered by life.

Lincoln's next political opportunity came in 1858. It was a chance he had hoped for—to unseat his political rival, Stephen A. Douglas, as senator from Illinois. In the aftermath of the Supreme Court's controversial Dred Scott decision of 1857, Lincoln's strategy was to depict his opponent as an oppressor of black Americans who favored the expansion of slavery into all Western territories.

By June of 1858 Lincoln won the Republican nomination for the Senate, and his acceptance speech, considered extreme in its sentiments, was viewed by many as an implied threat to resort to war as a necessary means of defeating slavery where it already existed. It stands as one of Lincoln's most famous orations:

> "A house divided against itself cannot stand."
>
> I believe this government cannot endure, permanently half slave and half free.
>
> I do not expect the Union to be dissolved—I do not expect the house to fall—but I do expect it will cease to be divided.
>
> It will become all one thing, or all the other.
>
> Either the opponents of slavery, will . . . place it where the public mind shall rest in the belief that it is in the course of ultimate extinction; or its advocates will put it forward, till it shall become alike lawful in all the States, old as well as new—North as well as South.

The 1858 Illinois senate campaign is today remembered for some of the most eloquent political debates ever staged. During the campaign, Douglas delivered more than 130 speeches, and Lincoln delivered more than 70. They also participated in seven face-to-face debates. In the 100 days before the election, Douglas traveled 5,227 miles and Lincoln traveled 4,350. Illinois proved itself to be the most interesting political battleground in the entire Union. People traveled by foot, carriage, horseback, and even canal boats to hear the two men speak. Special caravans of train cars were scheduled out of Chicago. Often the challenger would arrive in a procession of brass bands and military companies that stretched for nearly half a mile. Not to be outdone, Douglas often chose a princely carriage as his preferred means of transportation, which was led by four proud and spirited horses.

The candidates seldom disappointed their audience. Lincoln's words rang out as a testament to his belief in human equality and dignity: "This is a world of compensation, and he who would not be slave, must consent to have no slave. Those who deny freedom to others deserve it not for themselves." And he warned about the dangers of indifference or neutrality:

> Accustomed to trample on the rights of those around you, you have lost the genius of your own independence, and become the fit subjects of the first cunning tyrant who rises among you. And let me tell you that these things are prepared for you with the logic of history, if the elections shall promise that the next Dred Scott decision and all future decisions shall be acquiesced in by the people. . . . You can fool all the people some of the time, and some of the people all of the time, but you cannot fool all of the people all of the time.

Despite the keenness of his arguments, Lincoln failed to unseat his rival. Though disappointed with the outcome, he was not devastated because he realized that his audience had extended far beyond the boundaries of Illinois and that his words were heard and his insights shared by millions of Americans.

In the next two years, the power of the Republican Party increased rapidly, and by 1860 Republicans were confident their nominee would be placed in the White House after election day.

Good luck helped Lincoln become the nominee. Seward and Chase, candidates for the Republican presidential nomination in 1856, were the initial favorites. Lincoln was meeting with Republican officials at their Illinois convention in the small town of Decatur, a place he had passed through years earlier while on the trial circuit as an attorney. When Lincoln emerged from the meeting to greet the crowd outside, John Hanks, a cousin of his, pro-

A campaign poster for the Republican Party, featuring biographies of Lincoln and vice-presidential candidate Hannibal Hamlin, as well as the party's "platform," a description of Republican policies and principles. Lincoln received 1.9 million votes in the 1860 presidential election, defeating three other candidates.

ceeded to regale the crowd with an inspiring speech of how, 30 years earlier, he and his cousin, "honest Abe Lincoln," had split the rails that had built the house for his father, thereby conquering the wilderness and protecting him from the wolves of the forest. Now, claimed Hanks, the old rail splitter had returned, but this time he was looking to protect the people of Decatur from other, more dangerous enemies; namely, the people who were seeking to destroy the Union. The crowd went wild, and within a few weeks the rousing story of "Honest Abe Lincoln, the rail splitter" had spread all over the country.

At first glance, Lincoln seemed an unlikely candidate for president. He had little formal education, he was not wealthy, and he had never held any administrative positions in government. For the previous 10 years, in fact, he had not even held public offices of any kind. His entire national political career consisted of one undistinguished term as a congressman, and he held no ties to the political and economic establishment in the Eastern sections of the country. Furthermore, Lincoln had lost both of the Illinois state senatorial races in which he had participated, in 1855 and 1859.

However, Lincoln had a deep love and respect for the Constitution and the principles that it stood for, and rare levels of compassion, common sense, and intelligence. He was a vigorous, athletic man of inexhaustible energy and ideas. It was by this combination of qualities that the American public began to judge him, and not the ill-fitting clothes he wore, his ungainly physical appearance, or the clumsy way in which he carried himself. By late 1859, he had crossed much of the nation on a public-speaking tour and received positive receptions in Iowa, Ohio, Indiana, Kansas, and Wisconsin. Before the Republican convention, nearly every newspaper in the northern half of the country had favorable things to say about him. The *New York Tribune* even claimed, "He's the greatest man since St. Paul." Americans in the North came to see Lincoln as embodying virtues they believed the country was founded on: they viewed him as a hardworking, self-made man who was both a spokesman for the people of the West and an advocate of free soil. They respected him for having no bonds with the large financial concerns of the East.

Lincoln's victory in Chicago was not a total surprise, despite pre-convention sentiment that seemed to favor other Republicans heavily. The Republican delegates to the convention voted for a number of candidates, and no one candidate stood out after the first ballot. By the second ballot, Lincoln trailed Seward by only three votes, and momentum was clearly on his side. Realizing Lincoln's victory was inevitable, Seward advised all electors to cast their ballots for Lincoln, and "Honest Abe" left the city as the unanimous choice of his party.

A split in the Democratic Party helped Lincoln win the presidential election. One faction of Democrats nominated John Breckinridge, a Southerner; the other selected Lincoln's rival, Stephen Douglas. Douglas managed to attract some support in the South, but Breckinridge won majorities in all of the Southern states and attracted nearly 850,000 votes that might have allowed Douglas to win the election. Lincoln received approximately 1.9 million votes to Douglas's 1.4 million, as he defeated his political rival for the first time.

Before his train journey to Washington to assume leadership of a country marching toward civil war, Lincoln stopped by the law office in Springfield that he had shared with William Herndon for 16 years, to say good-bye. The two old companions looked back on the past and speculated on the future. As Lincoln viewed the name plate which read "Lincoln & Herndon" on the door for the last time, the soon-to-be president told his partner, "Let it hang there undisturbed. Give our clients to understand that the election of a President makes no change in the firm of Lincoln and Herndon. If I live I'm coming back some time, and then we'll go right on practicing as if nothing ever happened."

One month after Lincoln's inauguration, Rebel forces in South Carolina shelled Fort Sumter. After a two-day bombardment, the federal commander surrendered the fort on April 14, 1861. Lincoln responded to this aggression by calling for 75,000 militiamen to put down the rebellion in the Southern states.

5

THE DARKEST HOUR

AFTER LINCOLN'S ELECTION, the threat of war hung more heavily over the nation than ever before. Between the election in November 1860 and Lincoln's inauguration on March 4, 1861, seven Southern state legislatures voted to break away from the United States of America. "The Union is Dissolved!" proclaimed a banner headline in the *Charleston Mercury*. These states formed the Confederate States of America, drafted a constitution similar to the U.S. Constitution, and established a provisional government in Montgomery, Alabama. Militias in these Southern states seized federal forts and arsenals, forcing the Union troops to withdraw from the Confederate states.

In April of 1861, Lincoln faced his first challenge as president when the Confederates shelled Fort Sumter in Charleston harbor, South Carolina. After the Union commander surrendered the fort on April 14, cries for immediate revenge rippled through the North. Lincoln was not afraid to act, and he appealed to the loyal states for 75,000 militiamen. His plea was answered by 92,000 young men eager to punish the South for what was considered an act of war.

Citizens of border states were torn by the question of which side to choose. Kentucky, for instance, was the birthplace of both Lincoln and his Confederate counterpart, Jefferson Davis, president of the Confederate States of America, and it tried to remain neutral in the affair. Although the state eventually remained loyal to the Union, it did so only after Northern occupation of much of its territory. The eventual decision by Virginia to join the Confederacy proved particularly disheartening to Lincoln, as he had offered command of the Union forces to a brilliant military tactician, Robert E. Lee, who lived in an elegant estate in Arlington just across the Potomac from Washington, D.C. Lee's choice was an agonizing one, as his family had helped found the United States of America. He was the son of Lighthorse Harry Lee, a Revolutionary War hero, and a descendant of George Washington's wife's, Martha Custis Washington's, family. However, he felt that his loyalty to Virginia, his home state, was stronger than his loyalty to the United States, and he declined Lincoln's offer of command, instead taking control of the Army of Northern Virginia.

In addition to Virginia, other border states that joined the Confederacy were Arkansas, Tennessee, and North Carolina, while Kentucky was joined by Missouri, Maryland, and Delaware in the Union. Two years later Congress would admit the new state of West Virginia, composed of the western counties of Virginia where the residents were loyal to the Union, into the United States.

Both sides seemed confident of victory. The South had better generals, and its soldiers were fighting to defend their homeland and truly believed in the righteousness of their cause. The North, meanwhile, held a significant edge in raw materials and manufacturing capabilities, had three times as many miles of railroad, and had four times as many men available to fight.

But while the North did indeed possess enthusiasm, raw materials, and money, what it did not possess was a com-

Robert E. Lee was a highly respected U.S. Army general, and President Lincoln offered him command of the entire Union army at the outset of the Civil War. However, Lee felt his duty to Virginia, his home state, was greater than his duty to the nation, so he resigned his commission in the U.S. Army and took control of the Army of Northern Virginia.

petent general capable of leading men into battle. Realizing this, Lincoln concluded that he had "more holes than pegs to put in them" and immediately began his long, trying search for an inspired military leader. This lack of leadership was a problem that would continue to plague him for much of the war's duration. In fact, during the first two years of the war Lincoln was the Union's best military

These Union soldiers are relaxing near a pontoon bridge that the U.S. Army used to ford Bull Run, a small stream near Manassas Junction, Virginia. The federal army, confident of victory, was surprised and routed by Confederate forces at the Battle of Bull Run on July 21, 1861, the first major battle of the Civil War.

strategist. As Carl Shurz, later one of the nation's leading social reformers, wrote:

> He had great respect for other men's superior knowledge and higher culture, but these qualities did not make him afraid. In fact, he was afraid of no one and of nothing. . . . He was always able to recognize others' merits without being afraid thereby his own would be eclipsed. No problem, however important, could perplex him, for he judged all that came his way in accordance with the principles of ordinary logic and the rules of common sense. . . . Yet there could be no one more receptive of honest advice, or more tolerant of criticism. . . . If he was attacked or misunderstood, he would invite the objector to a friendly exchange of views, instead of breaking off relations.

Lincoln refused to recognize the right of the South to secede, and never referred to the armed conflict with the South as a civil war, but rather as a rebellion. This is not a minor distinction. In the event of a declared war, the U.S. Congress is responsible for the prosecution of the war, according to the Constitution of the United States. However, with a rebellion the responsibility falls to the nation's Chief Executive. Lincoln fulfilled this responsibility quite capably. In the upcoming months, it was Lincoln, and not a hesitant Congress, who extended the period of voluntary enlistment in the army from three months to three years, ordered a blockade of Southern ports, and mandated the purchase of wartime supplies with public funds. All of these decisions would prove critical in allowing the North to survive the early stages of the war, and all serve as tribute to the leadership of the man who ordered them.

Sounding more like a preacher than a president in his July 5, 1861, message to Congress, Lincoln argued that the coming struggle was nothing less than a struggle for the rights of man. Thus dignifying the war that was at hand, he told the Congress, "This is essentially a People's contest. On the side of the Union, it is a struggle for maintaining in the world, that form, and substance of government, whose leading object is, to elevate the conditions of man—to lift artificial weights from all shoulders—to clear the paths of laudable pursuit for all—to afford all, an unfettered start, and a fair chance, in the race of life." Once again he was choosing the moral high ground, and he was thus prepared to preserve a form of government that ensured the possibility of liberty and equality for individuals of all races. For Lincoln, there was much more at stake than the survival of the Union.

The first major battle of the war occurred on a dry summer day, July 21, 1861, behind a little stream called Bull Run, just 25 miles west of Washington, D.C. A carnival-like atmosphere surrounded the capital, and hundreds of citizens rode out to the site to picnic and view the entertainment of a one-battle war. They were joined by six U.S. senators, ten representatives, and reporters from scores of newspapers, who had all gathered to watch the hastily assembled Union army of 30,000 defeat the outnumbered Confederates under the leadership of General Pierre Beauregard. Even Lincoln was caught up in this wishful thinking—privately he hoped that General Irvin McDowell, the Union commander, would rout the Southern army and quickly march on to Richmond, the Southern capital.

The North's confidence quickly disappeared. The Southern army was able to check the Union offensive, and, led by a previously unknown general named Thomas Jackson, then hold their ground like a "stone wall," repelling a Union charge. The Confederates then counterattacked and forced the dispirited and exhausted Union army to flee the battlefield, joined in their retreat to Washington by the terrified citizens who had come out to witness a Union victory.

With the frightful realization that the struggle was to be a long one, Lincoln's political support quickly eroded. Even within his own party were heard the familiar accusations that the man in the White House was incompetent and that the events of the day were simply too big for a man who was at best ordinary.

Much of the anger directed at Lincoln stemmed from the seeming unpreparedness of the Union army, which was huddled around Washington to defend the capital from a Southern takeover of the city. Now under the leadership of General George B. McClellan, at first the sight of this growing army was greeted with admiration by the citizens of the area. Although McClellan had promised to reorganize the force, the 150,000-man army spent seven months in Washington, D.C., doing nothing. Because this army had been raised at considerable public expense, the sight of it lying idle on the banks of the Potomac began to offend and infuriate the citizens of the city. By January of 1862 the entire North puzzled about McClellan's inaction.

However, much of the public's hostility was not directed at the timidity of McClellan but rather at the man who had chosen him for the position. Ultimately, McClellan's inactivity proved to be as much a detriment to Lincoln as to the general himself—it raised the question to an apprehensive nation of whether Lincoln possessed the will to command. The initial answer seemed to be that he did not.

The war presented Lincoln with many other problems. The Mississippi River, the country's main transportation hub, was completely closed, and this shut out many of the nation's farmers from their markets. Issues such as tariffs, railroad charters, and the possible creation of an internal revenue system to finance the war provided a difficult legislative agenda before a Congress openly critical of Lincoln's leadership abilities. Opinion was even divided as

President Lincoln meets with General George B. McClellan and other generals of the Army of the Potomac in the summer of 1862. McClellan, who was appointed commander of the Union forces after the disastrous Battle of Bull Run, built a powerful fighting force of 150,000 well-trained soldiers; however, he refused to move his army against the Confederates. The delays frustrated Lincoln, who eventually had to directly order McClellan to advance his army.

Mary Todd Lincoln poses with her sons Willie (left) and Tad in 1860. Two years after this picture was taken, Willie died of typhoid fever. The loss of their child devastated the Lincolns.

to the actual prosecution of the war itself—some Republicans in Washington favored moderate policies that would not destroy the social fabric of the South, while other, more radical, members of Lincoln's party called for the South's complete destruction, along with the total emancipation of all slaves. No other president in the nation's history has been faced with more adversity.

Lincoln refused to allow McClellan to remain passive in engaging the enemy on the battlefield. Exasperated at the general's stalling tactics, on January 27, 1862, he published his "President's General War Order No. 1," in which he ordered the advance of all land and naval forces by the Union army within one month. In a thinly disguised attack on McClellan, the order held all generals personally accountable to the president if they failed to obey it.

For the North, this immediately affected the course of the war in a positive way. On February 6, General Ulysses S. Grant captured Fort Henry in Tennessee, and, less than two weeks later, Fort Donelson. On the 25th day of that month the Union army occupied Nashville, Tennessee. Lincoln was greatly encouraged by these events and once more hoped for an early end to the hostilities.

Personal tragedy, however, tempered his pleasure at these early successes. Due to a problem in the White House's water system, Lincoln's son Willie had fallen ill with a fever, believed to be typhoid, and for two weeks his condition steadily deteriorated. Finally, on February 20, 1862, the young boy succumbed to his illness. Both parents were left devastated by the untimely death of their young child. A melancholy Lincoln often locked himself into different rooms of the White House, where visitors and staff heard him weeping alone. Willie's death caused a depression that Lincoln would never be able to escape completely; long after Willie was buried, Lincoln often quoted a verse from *King John* in which Constance mourns the death of her son:

> And, father cardinal, I have heard you say
> That we shall see and know our friends in heaven:
> If that be true, I shall see my boy again.

Mary was even more crushed by the tragedy than her husband. In a state of total despair, she was bedridden for three months and could not even attend the funeral. Abraham was forced to hire a private nurse for her. She was so distraught from the tragic incident that never again would she be able to enter the room in which her son had died. The mood of the White House reflected that of its two primary tenants—for nearly a full year there were no social activities of any kind planned for the mansion of the first family.

With Willie's death also came the loss of any further optimism concerning the military course of the war. Union armies proved unable to sustain their earlier momentum in the West, and McClellan had once again resorted to a war of words rather than bullets. With Lincoln determined to advance on Richmond, the Confederate capital, McClellan's prolonged inactivity seemed to undermine the president's authority more than ever. The president grew so frustrated with his general that he even began referring to him as a traitor.

Another embarrassment for Lincoln was the mounting criticism he was forced to endure for his lack of success in attacking the institution of slavery. While he had urged Congress in March to adopt a resolution that offered the cooperation of the United States government to any state initiating the gradual abolishment of slavery, no Southern state ever accepted the offer of financial support promised by the measure. None, in fact, even considered the proposal. Soon the national praise for the resolution melted, and Lincoln was once again viewed as a man of few ideas who was unable to act on the few that he did have.

News from the front continued to disappoint the dejected president. On April 6, 1862, the army of Ulysses S. Grant was nearly routed in the small Kentucky town of Shiloh. However, amid the flowering shrubs and peach trees of the sleepy hamlet, Grant was able to push back the Rebel army the next day, but not before more than 13,000 soldiers of his force were killed, wounded, or taken prisoner. For Lincoln, even the news of Northern victories came tainted with stunning casualty reports. Shockingly, the total number of Americans (North and South) killed or wounded in this single encounter, 19,897, exceeded the total casualties of the American Revolution, War of 1812, and Mexican War combined. It was the costliest battle in

American history; bloodier battles were still to come.

By the summer of 1862, everything seemed to be going wrong for the North. General Robert E. Lee and his Army of Northern Virginia had forced McClellan's Army of the Potomac to retreat after the Seven Days' Battles, and this once again delayed Lincoln's plans for an offensive aimed at capturing Richmond.

During this time Lincoln was near exhaustion and couldn't sleep at night. He ate sparingly, if at all. In his own words, "Things had gone from bad to worse, until I felt that we had reached the end of our rope on the plan we had been pursuing . . . we had about played our last card, and must change our tactics, or lose the game." But

The bodies of Confederate soldiers lie in the sun along the Hagerstown Road after the battle of Antietam. The bloodiest one-day battle of the Civil War—over 22,000 Americans were killed, wounded, or captured—Antietam was technically a Union victory. However, General McClellan missed an opportunity to destroy the Confederate army by being too cautious.

This engraving, The First Reading of the Emancipation Proclamation, *shows Lincoln with his cabinet. Seated, left to right: Edwin M. Stanton, Abraham Lincoln, Gideon Welles, William Seward, Edward Bates; standing: Salmon P. Chase, Caleb Smith, and Montgomery Blair. Five days after the battle of Antietam, feeling that the tide of the war was turning, Lincoln announced his Emancipation Proclamation, which called for the freedom of all persons held as slaves in rebellious states on January 1, 1863.*

rhetoric did not translate into victories—in August of 1862 the North lost the second battle of Bull Run, and gloom completely enveloped the nation's capital. Every bed in Washington cradled the wounded, and deserters fleeing the call of duty filled the streets. The army itself was in a state of disorganized retreat. Lincoln was so upset by the turn of events in the city that even his faith that God was on his side was shaken. The downtrodden president claimed that "He permits (the war) for some wise purpose of his own, mysterious and unknown to us. . . . God's purpose is something different from the purpose of either party."

With Virginia free from Federal troops for the first time since the Civil War began, General Lee decided to take the offensive in September 1862. The Army of Northern Virginia invaded Maryland. Alarmed, Lincoln reinforced the Army of the Potomac and sent McClellan after the Confederate invaders.

The two armies met on September 17, 1862, at Antietam Creek. In an afternoon the participants thought would never end, the bone-weary and footsore soldiers of the Confederacy were able to force a standoff against an army that outnumbered them two to one. Although the battle of Antietam—the bloodiest one-day battle ever fought on U.S. soil—was technically a victory for McClellan, he passed up an opportunity to continue the fight and destroy Lee's army. McClellan's failure to press on for total victory infuriated the president; for Lincoln, it was the final straw. In November he removed McClellan from command and reassigned him to a recruiting post in New Jersey.

However, Lincoln turned the costly Union victory into a political success. Five days after the battle of Antietam, on September 22, 1862, Lincoln issued his preliminary Emancipation Proclamation, which called for the freedom of all persons held as slaves within any state still in rebellion as of January 1, 1863. To make the proclamation acceptable to Northern conservatives, Lincoln justified it as a "military necessity" to cripple Southern manpower. It did not free slaves in the border states, Tennessee, or parts of Virginia and Louisiana, because these areas were already under federal military control. Lincoln ordered this document to be officially published so that every citizen of the United States, both Union and Confederate, would be aware of his intentions.

Two days after its publication, the president still had doubts about his own wisdom and the clarity of his moral insights. Concerning what he himself would eventually consider the crowning achievement of his administration, Lincoln said, "I can only trust in God I have made no mistake. . . . It is now for the country and the world to pass judgement on. . . . I will say no more on the subject." He then added, "In my position I am environed with difficulties."

Though his plans for emancipation were enthusiastically supported by abolitionists in the North, the proclamation was predictably denounced by Southerners, and it sparked a renewal of their determination to win their war for independence. Cynical opponents of the proclamation pointed out that it didn't immediately free anyone—the slaves in the Southern states would not be freed without federal enforcement of the edict.

With the November congressional elections approaching, the president was aware of the potential liability his plans presented for the Republican Party. One visitor to the White House commented, "His introverted look and his half-staggering gait were like those of a man walking in his sleep." An old acquaintance who saw him at this time noted, "The change . . . was simply appalling. His whiskers had grown and had given additional cadaverousness to his face. . . . the light seemed to have gone out of his eyes, which were sunken far under his enormous brows. . . . There was over his whole face an expression of sadness, and a far-away look in the eyes, which was unlike the Lincoln of former days." The president's fears proved accurate—the Republican majority in Congress was drastically reduced after the election, and public ridicule of Lincoln continued to grow.

Lincoln's moral vision, however, failed to blur. In an address before Congress on December 1, 1862, the president delivered one of his most elegant and persuasive speeches. Urging his countrymen not to let the opportunity to end slavery and preserve the union escape, Lincoln declared:

> Fellow citizens, we can not escape history. We of this Congress and this administration will be remembered in spite of ourselves. . . . In giving freedom to the slave, we assure freedom to the free—honorable alike in what we give and what we preserve. We shall nobly save or meanly lose the last best hope on earth. Other means may suc-

During the first two years of the Civil War, Lincoln was unable to find a general capable of leading the Army of the Potomac against the Confederates. George McClellan (left) was a great organizer, but he was slow to attack, and his indecision on the battlefield allowed the Confederates to win battles despite being outnumbered. After his dismissal, Ambrose E. Burnside (top right) was appointed to command the Union armies, but he only lasted about a month and a half before being relieved of command after the disastrous federal loss at Fredericksburg in December 1862. After being appointed to lead the Union troops, "Fighting Joe" Hooker (bottom right) rebuilt the force and improved troop morale over the next four months. He led the Army of the Potomac on an offensive in April 1863, but was stopped at the battle of Chancellorsville when a surprise attack by the outnumbered Confederates under Robert E. Lee forced the Union Army to retreat.

ceed; this could not, can not fail. The way is plain, peace-
ful, generous, just—a way which, if followed, the world
will forever applaud, and God must forever bless.

Disastrously, less than two weeks later the Union Army
suffered its worst defeat ever. Commanded by General
Ambrose E. Burnside, who had replaced McClellan,
federal troops had marched across the icy Rappahannock
River to engage Lee's well-trained forces at Fredericksburg, Virginia. Lee had a strong position in the hills above
the city, and Confederate artillery and muskets found their
mark time after time as Burnside's Union army made a
series of frontal assaults, crossing a mile of open land to
try to reach the Confederate entrenchment. These coura-
geous assaults melted under Confederate firepower six
different times. By the time the final shot was fired, one in
ten Union soldiers was either dead, wounded, or missing.
As Burnside gave his final order to withdraw, he wept
openly at the casualties. The devastation was so great that
the victorious Lee concluded, "It is well that war is so terrible—[otherwise] we should grow too fond of it." A
reporter witnessing the battle wrote, "It can hardly be in
human nature for men to show more valor, or generals to
manifest less judgement."

Yet it was not Burnside who was blamed in the North,
but Lincoln. The *Chicago Tribune* editorialized, "Failure
of the army, weight of taxes, depreciation of money, waste
of cotton. . . . increasing national debt, deaths in the army,
no prospect of success, the continued closure of the Mississippi [River]. . . . all combine to produce the existing
state of dependency and desperation. The war is driving
toward a disastrous and disgraceful termination." The
harshest critics actually called for the president to resign.

Thus, as 1862 ended, there were few victories for the
administration to claim. Militarily, the North was bloodied
and outmaneuvered. With the forces in the East dead-
locked and no victories to report in the West in nearly half
a year, Union morale had reached a low point. Lincoln

was viewed as inept, and his announcement of emancipation had damaged him politically. The war itself presented
Lincoln with an unsolvable dilemma—some favored a
negotiated peace, others an even more forceful assault on
the rebel states.

But quitting was not part of Lincoln's nature. On
the eve of a new year, Abraham Lincoln would not
only endure, but prevail. His greatest moment was finally
at hand.

Abraham Lincoln in 1863, the turning point of the Civil War.

6

1863

THE PIVOTAL YEAR of the Civil War began with a festive New Year's reception at the White House attended by the president's cabinet and much of his diplomatic corps. The mood of gaiety inside the president's mansion contrasted with the somber decisions Lincoln had made in his first two years as president.

The first day of this new year was particularly special. Under the Emancipation Proclamation, nearly four million African-American slaves would be freed on January 1, 1863. By issuing the Emancipation Proclamation, Lincoln had raised the meaning of the Civil War from the suppression of a rebellion to that of a moral crusade.

Part of Lincoln's Proclamation reaffirmed the right of blacks to enroll in the armed forces, and for the North this paid immediate dividends. Within six months, black Americans would become key components in the Union armies in both the North and the West. By war's end, approximately 186,000 blacks would serve in the Union army under white officers, and more than 33,000 died for their country.

Another benefit of the Proclamation was the assistance it provided in halting foreign support for the South. Foreign countries such as England and France cut their ties with the Confederacy, because they did not want to be viewed as aiding a war fought for slavery. Some foreign diplomats even offered themselves as possible intermediaries in peace negotiations. Imperceptibly, the tide of the war had slowly turned against the Confederacy.

However, the effects of the Emancipation Proclamation would not be felt for several months, and as 1863 opened, Lincoln remained despondent over the direction the war had taken. The fragile state of his wife's mental health only added to his worries. Mary Todd Lincoln was still in mourning over the death of their son Willie and had taken to consulting with spiritualists, whom she believed communicated with him. She commonly held seances in the White House. Most disturbing for Lincoln was that Mary then came to believe that she too could communicate with both of her deceased children. She confided to her half-sister, "Willie lives. He comes to me every night and stands at the foot of the bed with the same sweet and adorable smile he always has had. . . . Little Eddie is sometimes with him." Mary's continuous emotional problems prevented her from providing Lincoln with support. He did, however, find refuge in the company of Tad, who always seemed to raise his spirits. Lincoln spent much time with Tad during this period of his life, and this provided some relief from the pressures of the war.

The first day of the new year also brought with it news of some negative developments from the front, as that day the federal garrison at Galveston, Texas, surrendered to the Rebel army. Midway through January, Lincoln relieved Burnside from command of the Army of the Potomac, replacing him with General Joseph Hooker, who began preparing the Union troops for a spring campaign into Virginia. Upon being named to command the Union army, "Fighting Joe" Hooker said, "May God have mercy on General Lee, for I will have none." Lincoln hoped this

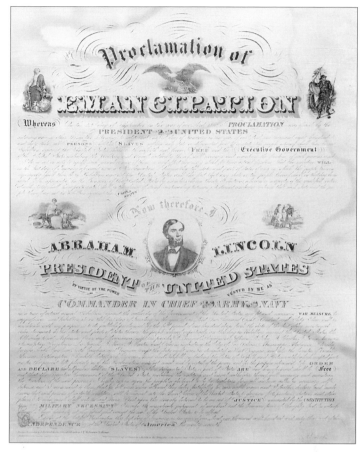

A copy of Lincoln's Emancipation Proclamation, issued on January 1, 1863. The proclamation helped the North's cause politically, as foreign nations withdrew their support for the South because they did not want to be viewed as pro-slavery.

would be the man who could lead the Union army to victory over the South.

In April, the 133,000-man Federal army marched into Virginia. Hooker divided his army into two equal forces, each larger than Lee's Army of Northern Virginia, and attempted to surround and destroy Lee's Confederates.

However, Lee realized Hooker's strategy and countered it with a surprise attack at Chancellorsville, Virginia. Lee's troops slammed into the men in blue with such furor that the undisciplined Union army simply panicked and ran. Though shielded by the cover of night, they still could not completely escape from their smaller enemy, as Lee's forces pressed their advantage. Hooker's army staged a

*Abraham Lincoln looks at an
album of Matthew Brady
photographs with his son, Tad.
During this trying time,
Lincoln found comfort in the
company of Tad.*

Abraham Lincoln looks at an album of Matthew Brady photographs with his son, Tad. During this trying time, Lincoln found comfort in the company of Tad.

wild three-day retreat, turning their backs to the onrushing Rebels. It was one of Lee's greatest victories, but also one of his costliest. Among the 1,600 Confederate soldiers killed on the battlefield was his brilliant associate, General Thomas "Stonewall" Jackson, who had accidentally been shot by one of his own men.

In the West, the Union forces under General Ulysses S. Grant had besieged one of the last remaining Confederate strongholds on the Mississippi River, the city of Vicksburg, Mississippi. Vicksburg stood on a bluff 200 feet above the river, and the Confederate army of 30,000 camped in the city had consistently managed to withstand Grant's continued assaults. Sensing that he was facing an impossible military situation, the general chose not to attack the elevated city at all, but rather to try and starve the Confederates into surrender.

Because the military situation of the North looked no

better in the first months of 1863 than it had in the first two years of the war, it is impressive that Lincoln was able to push several pieces of new legislation through Congress at this time. One of these new laws was the National Banking Act, which created a system of national banks to help finance the war. Another created the Department of Agriculture to assist the country's beleaguered farmers. Other legislation included the chartering of a transcontinental railroad and a conscription law which made all males between the ages of 20 and 45 subject to military service. By themselves, these programs represent an impressive legislative achievement, and the fact that Lincoln was able to accomplish so much in the middle of the war is even more remarkable. Amidst this flurry of legislation, the first half of the year drew to an end.

Following up on his victory at Chancellorsville in May, Lee had decided the Army of Northern Virginia should take the offensive, and his troops invaded Maryland and Pennsylvania in mid-June. Lincoln, frustrated with Hooker's caution in pursuing Lee, removed him from command of the army and replaced him with General George C. Meade, and the Army of the Potomac set out after Lee.

The handful of Confederate soldiers sent out in search of shoes in the small Pennsylvania town of Gettysburg on July 1, 1863, couldn't have realized at the time that they were setting the stage for what would prove to be the climactic battle of the war. While there, the Confederates skirmished briefly with some Union cavalrymen who had been separated from their main unit. The main Union force occupied wooded hills west of Gettysburg and held off the Confederate attack until reinforcements arrived.

For once, Lee was forced to fight on ground chosen by his opponent rather than himself. For the North this would prove to be an overwhelming tactical advantage that neither the brilliance of Lee nor the bravery of his men would be able to overcome.

The battle between the 76,000 gray-clad warriors of the

South and the 92,000 men in Union blue seesawed across the rolling green slopes for three agonizing days. The outcome of the battle seemed to hinge on every charge. On the third day of the battle, July 3, 1863, Lee was faced with two choices: admit failure and retreat, or try one last massive assault. The general ordered an attack on the center of the Union line. For nearly half a day Confederate cannons pounded the Union lines, hoping to weaken their will to fight, and then General George E. Pickett led 15,000 Rebel soldiers across a half-mile of open ground toward the Union position. The Union artillery had a clear view of the onrushing Southerners, and time after time cannons hit their mark. Those of Pickett's men who survived the cannon shells were then devastated by a solid wall of musket fire. One by one they fell, often on top of another dead body. Of the soldiers who started Pickett's Charge, barely half returned. Lee's army was defeated.

The Confederate loss at Gettysburg crippled the South's limited military manpower. Over 20,000 men were killed, wounded, or missing, and there were no more men of fighting age in the South to step in and take their places. The loss also left Lee emotionally battered. On the afternoon of July 4, 1863, the 87th birthday of the United States, the bloody, dejected Army of Northern Virginia retreated through a driving rain back to Virginia.

On the same day, more good news came for the North—the Confederate garrison at Vicksburg had surrendered. This divided the Confederacy and returned control of the Mississippi River to Union hands. The crippling defeats at Gettysburg and Vicksburg meant that the Southern armies would never assume the offensive again. The war had finally turned in favor of the North.

During the months that followed, the war's significance completely occupied Lincoln's thinking. With the Union victories at Gettysburg and Vicksburg, Northerners were convinced that the end was finally in sight and began to consider the fate of the South after the war's conclusion.

They debated on what terms the rebellious states should eventually be readmitted into the Union and began to ask themselves why exactly the war was fought in the first place. Lincoln, naturally, also thought of these issues, and he was urged by the national press to share his thoughts with his countrymen.

The opportunity to do so presented itself in November when Lincoln was invited to attend the dedication of a cemetery for the thousands of soldiers who had died at Gettysburg. Lincoln prepared his remarks very carefully and revised several drafts of the speech. In his first version, for instance, he wrote that the Declaration of Independence was penned "about eighty years ago," which he then changed to "fourscore and seven years ago." As he revised the text, he worried that the words he chose were incomplete and not worthy of the solemn occasion they would commemorate.

Lincoln shared his speech with no one before arriving

In June 1863, George Gordon Meade, who is standing in the center of this picture of his staff with both hands in his pockets, was appointed commander of the Army of the Potomac, replacing General Hooker. Meade moved his army to block Confederate General Lee's advance into the Northern states, and he met the Army of Northern Virginia at a small Pennsylvania town: Gettysburg.

A Confederate soldier lies dead behind a stone barricade near Little Round Top, a hill outside Gettysburg. The three-day battle was the highwater mark for the Confederacy, and marked the turning point in the Civil War. It was also one of the bloodiest battles: nearly 43,000 Union and Confederate soldiers were killed, wounded, or captured.

at the somber and almost eerie battlefield. He appeared lost in his own deep thoughts as Edward Everett, a former politician and the most famous orator of the day, spoke at the dedication for nearly two hours. A small black band fluttered from the stovepipe hat that he was wearing, indicating that he was still in mourning for his beloved son Willie. Appropriately enough, the color of the band matched the dark suit he wore.

As the president began to speak, many of those assembled to hear him appeared to have been distracted by a photographer attempting to capture the moment for future generations, and paid little or no attention to the words that were spoken. Perhaps they were expecting a speech as long as Everett's and were trying to seat themselves comfortably on the ground that now served as the final resting place for thousands.

Although it took only two minutes for Lincoln to give his speech, the words rang out with an enduring elegance. Commemorating those who had fallen in battle, Lincoln said:

Fourscore and seven years ago our fathers brought forth on this continent a new nation, conceived in liberty, and dedicated to the proposition that all men are created equal.

Now we are engaged in a great civil war, testing whether that nation, or any nation so conceived and so dedicated, can long endure. We are met on a great battle-field of that war. We have come to dedicate a portion of that field as a final resting place for those who here gave their lives that that nation might live. It is altogether fitting and proper that we should do this.

But in a larger sense, we can not dedicate—we can not consecrate—we can not hallow—this ground. The brave men, living and dead, have consecrated it far above our poor power to add or detract. The world will little note, nor long remember what we say here, but it can never forget what they did here. It is for us, the living, rather, to be dedicated here to the unfinished work which they who fought here have thus far so nobly advanced. It is rather for us to be here dedicated to the great task remaining before us—that from these honored dead we take increased devotion to that cause for which they gave the last full measure of devotion—that we here highly resolve that these dead shall not have died in vain—that this nation, under God, shall have a new birth of freedom—and that government of the people, by the people, for the people, shall not perish from the earth.

While mentioning neither the battle of Gettysburg itself nor the two armies that met there, Lincoln decided to address the larger issues of the Civil War, and by so doing he defined forever exactly why it was being fought. Five times in his 272-word address he used the word "nation," reflecting his deep belief that the United States was more than just a loose union of free and independent states. Of

> Four score and seven years ago our fathers brought forth, upon this continent, a new nation, conceived in Liberty, and dedicated to the proposition that all men are created equal.
>
> Now we are engaged in a great civil war, testing whether that nation, or any nation, so conceived, and so dedicated, can long endure. We are met here on a great battle-field of that war. We have come to dedicate a portion of it as a final resting place for those who here gave their lives that that nation might live. It is altogether fitting and proper that we should do this.

A handwritten excerpt from Lincoln's Gettysburg Address. Lincoln's brief speech at the dedication of the Gettysburg National Cemetery in November 1863 addressed what he believed to be the most important reason the Civil War was being fought—to preserve the United States.

critical importance is Lincoln's belief that the nation grew from the Declaration of Independence in 1776 and not the ratification of the Constitution in 1787—Lincoln was appealing to the idea that it was the union created by the individual states, and not the states themselves, that would prevail in the long run. His reference to the Declaration was also a symbolic one, as its stirring announcement of the equality of man was a powerful condemnation of the inherent evils of slavery. Lincoln's brief Gettysburg Address ranks as one of the greatest speeches ever made by an American president.

As the year came to a close, the military news became more encouraging for the North. After his victory at Vicksburg, Grant won a series of engagements in the vicinity of Chattanooga, Tennessee, and he began to formulate plans for an invasion of Georgia with General William T. Sherman. The Southern army had now retreated to defensive positions.

In November that year the president proclaimed the last Thursday of that month as the first national day of Thanksgiving; this can be seen as a reflection of the optimism he was feeling as the year drew to a close. On December 9, in his annual message to Congress, Lincoln revealed his generous visions of a post-war America, in which he called for a "full pardon . . . with restoration of all rights of property, except as to slaves" to all Southerners, except high Confederate government officials. He then promised to extend full political recognition to all states when new governments were approved by ten percent of their residents. Lincoln's plans for amnesty and reconstruction represented extremely lenient conditions for Southern states to be readmitted into the Union, and they displeased many radical Northerners who were determined to punish the South for its offenses. But Lincoln was more interested in forgiving than condemning, and more interested in healing than wounding in revenge, and he would have none of this thinking. For the president, 1863 ended with hope.

Abraham Lincoln's face shows the ravages of four years of bloody civil war. This photo was taken in April 1865, a few days before Lincoln was assassinated.

7

"WE WILL GO BACK TO ILLINOIS"

ALTHOUGH NO AMERICAN president had been elected to a second term since Andrew Jackson in 1832, Lincoln spoke openly of his desire to complete his unfinished work as early as the fall of 1863. However, even with the end of the war in sight, his chances seemed slim.

Abolitionists were distraught because he had failed to eliminate slavery completely. Throughout the North, there was some discontent that its 20 million citizens still could not find a way to defeat the 4 million people of the South after nearly three years of bloody warfare. This uneasiness with Lincoln's policies was caused by the unfavorable turn of events in the winter of 1863–64, as the Northern armies were unable to sustain the momentum of their victories the previous summer and fall and seemed stalemated once again. To replenish the dwindling Union forces, Lincoln ordered 500,000 more men into the army on February 1, 1864. Less than two months later, he increased this by 200,000, which sparked outrage in the national press. "The people have lost all confidence in his ability to suppress the rebellion and restore the Union," chimed one publication, which added that the reason for this was the "indecision of the President," the "feebleness of his will," and his "want of intellectual grasp." But Lincoln silenced his critics when, on March 8, 1864, in an effort to speed up the war's end, he summoned Ulysses S. Grant to Washington and named him the new general-in-chief of the Federal armies.

Grant immediately inaugurated a single chain of command for all Union armies to obey, which would allow them to follow a single coordinated plan of battle. He tried to maneuver Lee into an open battle where he could possibly put him away once and for all. Lee, recognizing the numerical superiority of the North, declined to meet the Union army in a major battle, opting instead for a series of smaller encounters. The strategy almost worked for the Southerner. Yet despite the staggering losses suffered by the Union army, at the end of the campaign Grant's army was larger than when it started, while Lee's was dramatically smaller. Lincoln's call-up of additional manpower was reaping significant rewards.

The springtime successes on the battlefield did not go unnoticed in the country's newspapers, and for once it was Lincoln who received most of the praise. His campaign for reelection received solid editorial support from Maine ("The feeling for Lincoln is very strong here," wrote one newspaper) to California ("Lincoln is the choice of the people overwhelmingly!," said another editorial). The candidate grew more and more confident of his chances for reelection. This confidence, however, was short lived. A series of nearly inexplicable losses jolted the president, who was officially renominated by the Republican party in June. At Kennesaw Mountain in Georgia, the army of William Sherman was bloodily defeated, and in Virginia, Benjamin Butler's troops were trapped on a peninsula between the James and Appomattox Rivers. Also in Virginia, Lee dealt his arch-rival Grant a stunning defeat, due in large part to an ill-advised and doomed charge by the Northerner at Cold Harbor. After viewing the carnage, a

General Ulysses S. Grant, whose capture of Vicksburg brought control of the Mississippi River into federal hands, was appointed commander of the Union armies in March 1864.

shaken Grant commented, "Without a greater sacrifice of human life than I am willing to make, all cannot be accomplished that I had designed." Where was the victory over the South that had seemed so certain just a few months earlier?

By mid-1864, demands for a negotiated end to the war were growing louder and louder. The Democrats, who nominated Lincoln's former general, George McClellan, as their presidential candidate, adopted a peace platform at their convention in Chicago in August, and this was widely hailed by scores of Northerners. In the Republican Party, some felt Lincoln's plans to readmit the Southern

Troops commanded by General William T. Sherman marched through the South, destroying the Confederacy's transportation and communication facilities and with them the rebels' ability to wage war. These troops are tearing up tracks in Atlanta before starting on the "March to the Sea."

states to the Union (called Reconstruction) were too lenient; others thought his methods too severe.

Further complicating matters, the military stalemate continued. In July, an advancing Rebel army imperiled the city of Washington, and government clerks were issued rifles to defend the capital. The president ordered a naval vessel moored in the Potomac in case it was needed to move himself and his family to safety in the event of a Union evacuation of the city. And on July 30, 1864, when citizens of Chambersburg, Pennsylvania, could not meet Southern ransom demands of $100,000 in gold and $500,000 in currency, the Confederates burned the city to the ground. The entire North was not only frustrated, it was also humiliated. How could victory prove so elusive?

Lincoln, though, refused bow to his critics. In August he ordered the Treasury to announce a new $200 million loan to finance the war, and he made plans to draft an additional 400,000 men into the army in September. That same month, when Democratic candidate McClellan declared the war a failure, Lincoln refused to even acknowledge him.

Good news finally came in August and September. Rear Admiral David Farragut captured Mobile Bay on August 5, 1864, bringing all the major Confederate ports on the Gulf of Mexico under Union control. More good news followed—from Georgia, deep in the heart of the Confederacy, General Sherman informed the president that "Atlanta is ours." His troops had captured the city after four months of fighting.

These stunning and potentially decisive military victories spelled doom for Democrats at the polls, and they were reduced to attacks on Lincoln's character in their desperate attempt to unseat him. Despite predictions of a close election, Lincoln led his party to a huge victory, winning an impressive 55 percent of the popular vote and 212 electoral votes to McClellan's 21. The President's reelection signaled the day when slavery would once and forever be abolished in the United States and the Union would be reconstructed. Lincoln's subsequent demand for passage of the 13th Amendment ensured the legal abolishment of slavery.

As he prepared to deliver his second inaugural speech, the president was advised to increase his security precautions. With military defeat a likelihood for the South, there were some angry and desperate Southerners who felt that the only remaining alternative for them was the assassination of the head of the Northern armies.

This was not an entirely new fear—ever since Lincoln's first inauguration he had been receiving threats on his life.

But Lincoln believed that as president he should not be screened from the people who elected him, and he tended to ignore these threats. "It would never do for a President to have guards with drawn sabres at his door," he claimed, "as if he fancied he were, or were trying to be, or were assuming to be, an emperor." Lincoln felt that if someone were trying to kill him, "no vigilance could keep them out. . . . A conspiracy to assassinate, if such there were, could easily obtain a pass to see me for any one or more of the instruments." Yet with his reelection, both embittered Southerners and frustrated Northerners realized that the policies of the Lincoln administration would continue for another four years, and rumors of a plot to assassinate the president were heard with increasing frequency. Shockingly, it was an idea that was even endorsed by a small element of the national press: "And if he is elected . . . for another four years, we trust some bold hand will pierce his heart with dagger point for the public good," proclaimed the *La Crosse (Wisconsin) Democrat* months before the election. In this type of atmosphere, security around the president increased at the start of his second term, despite Lincoln's objections.

During the four months between the election and the inauguration, developments on the battlefield continued in such a positive direction for the North that victory seemed more certain than ever before. By December 1864, Grant had pinned Lee down in Virginia, and on Christmas Day Sherman wired the president from Georgia with welcome news: "I beg to present you, as a Christmas gift, the city of Savannah, with 150 heavy guns and plenty of ammunition, and also about 25,000 bales of cotton." With the Southern armies defeated in Tennessee and battered in Virginia, and with Union troops marching virtually unopposed through South Carolina, Lincoln, for the first time, was able to rejoice with the realization that peace was finally at hand.

He busied himself with his plans for reuniting his

WE WILL GO BACK TO ILLINOIS

nation divided by four years of Civil War. Lincoln slowly began to push for Negro suffrage, believing it to be the best hope for the freed former slaves to protect their rights in the South. He also lobbied for policies that would welcome the Southern states back into the Union and begin the process of healing immediately. Congress was largely receptive to his proposals, realizing that it was unwise to oppose a president who had recently won his reelection by such an impressive margin. The national press was also on his side. Chimed the *New York Herald*: "This extraordinary rail-splitter enters upon his second term the unprecedented master of the situation in reference to American affairs, at home and abroad."

It was hope that shaped the words of Lincoln's Second Inaugural Address on March 4, 1865, which spoke of the prospect of unquestioned forgiveness and the promise of

Pursued by Union armies, General Lee surrendered his Army of Northern Virginia to General Grant on Sunday, April 9, 1865, at Appomattox Court House in Virginia. Although some rebel forces continued to fight in the West for several months, Lee's surrender marked the end of the Confederacy.

John Wilkes Booth, a well-known actor, was one of a group of Southern sympathizers who were plotting to kill the leaders of the federal government. Booth was the only one to complete his assignment, shooting Lincoln while the president was watching a play in Ford's Theater on the evening of April 14, 1865. Booth was later hunted down and killed in Maryland. A number of the other conspirators were arrested, tried, and hung (right) for their involvement in the plot.

national rebirth. The capital was filled for the occasion. On a morning that was wet and windy, crowds gathered before the podium for more than two hours before Lincoln was to speak. As the president rose from his seat to be sworn in, cheers erupted from the crowd, the band struck up a lively tune, and the American flag was waved. Symbolically, just as he was about to speak, the sun broke through the clouds and shone on the man who had endured unimaginable personal tragedies to lead his country to its greatest triumph.

In typical Lincoln fashion, he spoke briefly, only 703 words, but the speech he delivered is one of his most memorable. Of the war that was now ending, Lincoln said, "All dreaded it—all sought to avert it." While never men-

tioning the South or the Confederacy by name, he then added that one of the parties "would make war rather than let the nation survive, and the other would accept war rather than let it perish. And the war came." As for its reason, Lincoln claimed that slavery was "somehow, the cause of the war." But he then continued on his theme of unity rather than division and forgiveness rather than resentment in his claim that the citizens of the United

States "read the same Bible, and pray to the same God, and each invoke this aid against the other. . . . Let us judge not that we be not judged." Why did the war last for such an eternity? Because "the Almighty has His own purposes," Lincoln said, absolving both sides of guilt for their role in the conflict. He then combined his hope for the future of his country—"fondly do we hope—fervently do we pray—that this mighty scourge of war may speedily pass away"—with his determination to bring the war to a just end—"Yet, if God wills that it continue, until all the wealth piled by the bond-man's two hundred and fifty years of unrequited toil shall be sunk, and until every drop of blood drawn with the lash, shall be paid by another drawn with the sword, as was said three thousand years ago, so still must be said, 'The judgements of the Lord, are true and righteous altogether.'" He then concluded his remarks: "With malice toward none; with charity toward all; with firmness in the right as God gives us to see the right, let us strive on to finish the work we are in; to bind up the nation's wounds; to care for him who shall have borne the battle, and for his widow, and his orphan, to do all which may achieve and cherish a just and lasting peace among ourselves, and with all nations."

A month after the inauguration, on the night of April 9, 1865, Lincoln received the news that Lee had surrendered to Grant at Appomattox Court House in Virginia. Early the next morning, the citizens of the capital awoke to the sound of 500 cannons announcing the news to the entire country. A huge throng of celebrants immediately descended upon the White House and demanded to hear from the president. When Tad Lincoln appeared, waving a flag from a second floor window, they erupted in a wild and prolonged cheer.

The next day, April 11, there was a huge celebration throughout all of Washington. Government buildings and private homes left their lights burning all through the night, and the dome of the Capitol could be seen for miles.

Thousands of celebrants assembled in front of the White House, and once again they demanded an appearance from the president. This time Lincoln obliged, giving a brief speech about his plans for leniency toward the defeated South.

Not everyone, however, was cheering for Lincoln. In the crowd that night was at least one man not sharing in the festive atmosphere that had taken over the capital. His name was John Wilkes Booth.

A 26-year-old actor and the brother of a famous stage star, Edwin Booth, John Wilkes Booth was rabidly loyal to the South. A racist who firmly believed that the United States was formed only for the benefit of white men, Booth also harbored deep personal resentment of President Lincoln, not only because of the war but also—since Booth considered himself a Southern aristocrat—for his plain appearance and lack of sophistication. Booth viewed Lincoln as a tyrant and was committed to helping his beloved South in whatever way possible. As the president urged black voting rights outside the White House that night, Booth was enraged. "That is the last speech he will ever make," he vowed as he stalked off into the night.

At a cabinet meeting on Friday, April 14, Lincoln expressed his optimism for reuniting his beloved country. He once again repeated his plans for leniency: "I hope there will be no persecutions, no bloody work after the war is over. None need expect me to take any part in hanging or killing them. . . . Enough lives have been sacrificed. We must extinguish our resentment if we expect harmony and union." The meeting ended successfully, and those who attended it reported that the president was in great spirits. Concluding his afternoon with the routine affairs of his office, he had an early dinner with Mary because of their plans to attend the theater that evening.

On their ride to the theater Lincoln was still in an extremely upbeat mood, confiding to his wife that, after his term was finished, "We will go back to Illinois and

Lincoln's statue is in the central chamber of the Lincoln Memorial, which was built in Washington, D.C., in 1922. The inscription behind Lincoln's head reads, "In this temple, as in the hearts of the people for whom he saved the Union, the memory of Abraham Lincoln is enshrined forever."

pass the rest of our lives in quiet."

When Abraham and Mary Lincoln entered Ford's Theater at 8:30 P.M., the band played "Hail to the Chief!" and the audience rose and cheered. Lincoln smiled. The play that evening had been written by an Englishman and was titled *Our American Cousin.*

At 10:13 P.M., John Wilkes Booth entered the president's box. From a distance of two feet, he pulled the trigger of his derringer pistol and fired a shot into the back of Lincoln's head. The president slumped forward in his seat. Through the long night that followed, he would never regain consciousness. His disconsolate wife sat at his bedside, first urging him to speak to her, then asking him to take her along with him. The president's breathing grew fainter and fainter. At 7:22 on the morning of April 15, Lincoln's heart stopped forever, and the physician informed his wife, "It is all over. The President is no more."

After a funeral service in the White House, Lincoln's body was taken back to Illinois on a long funeral train, retracing the route Lincoln had taken to Washington before his first inauguration. Thousands of sorrowful people lined the tracks to watch as the train slowly passed.

Although Abraham Lincoln was dead, his dream of freedom for all Americans still lived. On December 18, 1865, the 13th Amendment to the Constitution was passed into law, ending slavery in the United States forever. On July 28, 1868, the 14th Amendment to the Constitution was passed, which granted to all people born or naturalized in the United States the right of citizenship. On March 30, 1870, the 15th Amendment to the Constitution was passed. No longer could any man in the United States be denied his right to vote because of the color of his skin.

These amendments stand as Abraham Lincoln's greatest triumphs and as indelible proof of his courage and moral convictions. With the preservation of the Union and its enduring promise of freedom and equality to all Americans, Abraham Lincoln still lives in the hearts of all people dedicated to the ideal of human equality.

APPENDIX A

MARY TODD LINCOLN'S MENTAL PROBLEMS

SOME HISTORIANS believe that Mary Todd Lincoln was mentally unbalanced for most of her marriage to Abraham Lincoln. Although she was an intelligent, vivacious young woman by all accounts, after her marriage Mrs. Lincoln's personality began to change. This may have been in part because Lincoln was unable to support his young bride in the manner to which she had become accustomed as a Southern belle. Lincoln's frequent absences from home while traveling through Illinois practicing law probably also contributed to her mental problems.

And although Mary was proud of her husband, their marriage was filled with tragedy. Mrs. Lincoln was devastated by the deaths of her two sons, Edward in 1850 at age 4 and 12-year-old William in 1862 at the height of the Civil War. The assassination of her husband as he was seated next to her in Ford's Theater took a further toll. Observers from the time say she was never quite sane again after April 15, 1865.

After her husband's death, she became obsessively concerned about her financial future. Fearful of going into debt, she sold her clothing and many belongings, an action that caused a public uproar. Actually, she had an annual income that was enough to support her lifestyle. In addition to the proceeds from Lincoln's estate, Congress had granted her an annuity of $3,000 (increased to $5,000 in 1880).

Meanwhile, the death of another child, 18-year-old Thomas (Tad), in 1871 further unbalanced her. By 1875, Mary Lincoln's mental state had become so bad that her remaining living son, Robert Todd Lincoln, was afraid she would commit suicide. He had her declared insane and committed to a private sanatorium. She remained there for four months

Mary Todd Lincoln struggled with mental illness for much of her life.

before being released into the care of her sister, Elizabeth Edwards, in Springfield, Illinois. (It was this sister that Mary Todd had been living with when she first met and fell in love with young Abraham Lincoln in 1840.)

Mary Todd Lincoln lived in Europe for the next four years, returning to the United States in 1880. Her health was poor for the last six years of her life, and she died in Springfield on July 16, 1882.

APPENDIX B

THE PLOT TO ASSASSINATE LINCOLN

LATE IN 1864, even the most fanatical Confederate sympathizers could see that a Union victory was inevitable. However, some rebels felt that if they could destroy the structure of the federal government, a new administration would not have the stomach to continue the war and would allow the Southern states to secede from the United States of America.

One of the men who believed this was a 26-year-old actor named John Wilkes Booth. Booth's father, Junius Brutus Booth, was a great Shakespearean actor, and his brother, Edwin Booth, is considered the greatest American actor of the 19th century. Booth himself was a talented actor, but unlike the rest of his family he supported the Confederate attempt at secession.

In 1864 Booth plotted to kidnap President Lincoln, planning to ransom him for Confederate prisoners. While he was living at Mary Surratt's boardinghouse in Washington, D.C., in late 1864, other Confederate sympathizers were recruited to help carry out the plot. These included former Confederate soldiers Samuel Arnold and Michael O'Laughlin; Mary Surratt's son, John, a Confederate spy; George Atzerodt, a carriage maker; David Herold; and Lewis Payne.

The group originally planned to seize Lincoln at Ford's Theater on January 18, 1865, but the president did not come to the performance that night. On another occasion, the conspirators stopped Lincoln's carriage while it was traveling around Washington, D.C., but Lincoln was not inside and the plotters scattered in disarray.

After the kidnap plan failed, and with the hopes of the South failing as well, Booth decided on a darker, more complex scheme: assassinate

Lewis Payne attempted to kill William Seward, the U.S. Secretary of State, on the night President Lincoln was assassinated. Although he was able to stab Seward, the wound was not fatal. Payne was hanged with other conspirators in the assassination plot on July 7, 1865.

the president, the vice president, and the other top government officials who were members of Lincoln's cabinet. Booth planned to kill the president, and he directed Atzerodt to assassinate Vice President Andrew Johnson. Payne was directed to kill Secretary of State William H. Seward. Some historians believe another assassin was sent to kill General Ulysses S. Grant, but an attempt on his life was never made.

Shortly after 10 p.m. on April 14, Booth entered the back of the president's box at Ford's Theater, where Abraham and Mary Lincoln were watching *Our American Cousin*. He held a single-shot derringer to the back of the president's head and fired, then leapt from the box to the stage. He landed badly and broke his left leg. Hobbling through the stunned actors, he shouted "Sic semper tyrannis!" ("Thus ever to tyrants!") and escaped.

Tragically, Booth's assassination attempt was a success. Lincoln never recovered, and he died at 7:22 a.m. Saturday, April 15, without regaining consciousness.

The other conspirators, however, were less successful. Atzerodt never made an attempt to kill the vice president, and although Payne was able to stab Secretary of State Seward, the wound was not fatal.

After the assassination, Booth and Herold escaped to Maryland, where Booth's broken leg was set by Dr. Samuel Mudd. The pair then continued south, hiding from the federal troops searching for Lincoln's murderer.

The nation was angered at Lincoln's assassination, and Secretary of War Edwin M. Stanton wasted no time in taking action. He directed the search for Booth and Herold, and also rounded up the other conspirators: Atzerodt, Payne, O'Laughlin, Arnold, and Edward Spangler, a stagehand at Ford's Theater who had helped Booth escape after Lincoln's assassination. Mary Surratt, the woman who owned the boarding house where the conspiracy had been hatched, was also arrested, although her son John eluded capture for nearly two years. Although Dr. Mudd was not involved in Booth's plot, he was also arrested because he had assisted the escaping assassin.

On April 26, Booth and Herold were surrounded in a barn near Port Royal, Virginia. Herold surrendered, and when Booth refused to give up, the soldiers set the barn on fire. Booth was killed by a bullet to the back of the neck, but no one is certain who fired the fatal shot.

A trial for the other conspirators, before a military commission rather than a civilian jury, was held from May 9 to June 30, 1865. Arnold, O'Laughlin, and Mudd received life sentences; Mrs. Surratt, Payne, Atzerodt, and Herold were sentenced to be hanged. Spangler received a six-year sentence. Mrs. Surratt, Payne, Atzerodt, and Herold were hanged on July 7, 1865, and the others were imprisoned at Fort Jefferson, Florida. O'Laughlin died in prison of yellow fever in 1867, and Arnold, Mudd, and Spangler were pardoned by President Johnson in 1869. John Surratt was tried in 1867 and freed by a hung jury.

APPENDIX C

CIVIL WAR ASSOCIATIONS

The following is a list of organizations that are involved with preserving Civil War history.

The U.S. Civil War Center
David Madden, Director
Louisiana State University
Baton Rouge, LA 70803
504-388-3151
http://www.cwc.lsu.edu

The American Civil War Institute
Kent Masterson Brown, Director
Campbellsville University
1 University Drive
Campbellsville, KY 42718-2799
800-264-6014

Civil War Institute
Tina M. Grim, Program Manager
Gettysburg College
Campus Box 435, 233 North
    Washington St.
Gettysburg, PA 17325
717-337-6590
http://www.gettysburg.edu/
    ~tgrim/cwi_tina.html
tgrim@gettysburg.edu

Association for the Preservation of Civil War Sites, Inc.
11 Public Square, Suite 200
Hagerstown, MD 21740
301-665-1400
http://www.apcws.com
apcws@intrepid.net

George Tyler Moore Center for the Study of the Civil War
Shepherd College
Shepherdstown, WV 25443
304-876-5429
http://www.shepherd.wvnet.edu/
    gtmcweb/cwcenter.htm

Sons of Union Veterans of the Civil War (SUVCW)
Richard D. Orr, Commander in Chief
153 Connie Dr.
Pittsburgh, PA 15214-1251
home: 412-931-1173
work: 412-578-8055
SUVCWORR@aol.com
http://suvcw.org/

Sons of Confederate Veterans International Headquarters
PO Box 59
Columbia, TN 38402-0059
1-800-MY-SOUTH or
    1-800-MY-DIXIE

CHRONOLOGY

1809   Born Abraham Lincoln on February 12 in Kentucky

1818   Abraham's mother, Nancy, dies; Thomas Lincoln marries Sarah Bush Johnson the next year

1834   Elected to the Illinois state legislature as a Whig candidate

1837   Moves to Springfield, Illinois, and opens a law practice with John Stuart

1840   Meets Mary Todd in Springfield

1842   Marries Mary Todd

1843   The Lincoln's first child, Robert, is born

1845   A second child, Edward, is born

1846   Elected to the U.S. House of Representatives

1850   Four-year-old Edward Lincoln dies; Congress passes legislation, known as the "Compromise of 1850," intended to prevent Southern secession from the United States; William Lincoln is born

1853   The Lincoln's fourth son, Thomas (Tad) is born on April 4

1854   Congress passes the Kansas-Nebraska Act, which allows new territories to determine by "popular sovereignty" whether or not to permit slavery; the Republican Party is formed to oppose slavery in new territories

1858   Lincoln gains national prominence as a politician despite losing election for the U.S. Senate to incumbent Stephen Douglas

1860   Elected 16th president of the United States

1861   On April 12 Confederates shell the federal arsenal at Fort Sumter, South Carolina—the first shots of the Civil War; Confederates win early battle by routing the Union Army at Bull Run

1862   William Lincoln dies at age 12; Union army defeats Confederates at the battle of Antietam; Lincoln announces his intention to free slaves in rebellious territories

1863   Lincoln signs the Emancipation Proclamation, abolishing slavery; the Army of Northern Virginia is defeated at the battle of Gettysburg, marking a turning point in the war

1864   Lincoln appoints Ulysses S. Grant to command the Union armies; wins second term as president

1865   General Robert E. Lee surrenders his Confederate Army to Ulysses S. Grant at Appomattox Court House on April 9; Lincoln is assassinated by John Wilkes Booth at Ford's Theater on April 14, and dies the next morning

FURTHER READING

Baker, Jean H. *Mary Todd Lincoln: A Biography*. New York: Norton, 1987.

Bruns, Rodger. *World Leaders Past and Present: Lincoln*. Philadelphia: Chelsea House Publishers, 1986.

Donald, David Herbert. *Lincoln*. New York: Simon & Schuster, 1995.

Handlin, Oscar. *Abraham Lincoln and the Union*. Boston: Little, Brown, 1980.

Ludwig, Emil. *Lincoln*. Boston: Little, Brown, and Co., 1930.

McPherson, James M. *Battle Cry of Freedom: The Civil War Era*. New York: Oxford University Press, 1988.

Oates, Stephen B. *Abraham Lincoln: The Man Behind the Myths*. New York: Harper & Row, 1984.

Stephenson, Nathaniel Wright, ed. *The Autobiography of Abraham Lincoln—Consisting of the Personal Portions of his Letters, Speeches, and Conversations*. Indianapolis: The Bobbs-Merrill Company, 1926.

Tindall, George B., and David E. Shi. *America*. New York: W. W. Norton & Co., 1984.

INDEX

Abolitionism, 13, 14, 31, 39, 41, 49, 69, 87
African Americans, 12, 51, 75, 93, 97, 99. *See also* Slavery
American System, 41-42
Antietam, battle of, 68-69

Beauregard, Pierre, 62
Bell, John, 17
Black Hawk War, 27
Booth, John Wilkes, 97, 98-99
Breckinridge, John C., 17, 55
Brown, John, 14-15
Buchanan, James, 18
Burnside, Ambrose E., 70, 72, 76

California gold rush, 42
Chase, Salmon P., 50, 52
Civil War, 12, 21, 31, 57-96
Clay, Henry, 28, 41-42
Compromise of 1850, 14, 46-47
Confederate States of America, 17, 57-64, 66-96
Constitution, U.S., 14, 31, 39, 54, 57, 61, 84, 91, 99

Davis, Jefferson, 17, 58
Dayton, William, 50
Declaration of Independence, 48, 81, 84

Democratic party, 15, 29, 49, 55, 89, 91
Department of Agriculture, U.S., 79
Donald, David Herbert, 41
Douglas, Stephen, 15, 16, 50-52, 55

Emancipation Proclamation, 69-70, 72, 75-76
Everett, Edward, 82

Farragut, David, 91
Fifteenth Amendment, 99
Fourteenth Amendment, 99
Franklin, Benjamin, 26
Fremont, John C., 50
Fugitive Slave Act, 47

Gettysburg, battle of, 79-80, 83
Gettysburg Address, 81-85
Grant, Ulysses S., 65, 66, 78, 85, 88, 89, 92, 96

Hanks, John, 52
Harper's Ferry raid, 14-15
Herndon, William, 33, 55
Hooker, Joseph, 76-78

Illinois, 27, 36, 40, 49, 50, 51, 52, 54, 99
Illinois House of Representatives, 48
Illinois state legislature,

28, 36
Indiana, 25, 26

Jackson, Andrew, 28, 87
Jackson, Thomas "Stonewall," 62, 78
Jefferson, Thomas, 48

Kansas, 14, 47
Kansas-Nebraska Act, 47
Kennedy, John F., 23
Kentucky, 23, 38, 58

Lee, Robert E., 58, 66, 68, 72, 76-80, 88, 92, 96
Lincoln, Abraham
    assassination, 20, 91-92, 97-99
    birth, 23
    childhood, 23-27
    in Congress, 37-41
    early jobs, 27-28, 40
    education, 16, 23-24, 26, 27, 36, 50, 54
    and Emancipation Proclamation, 69-70, 72, 75-76
    and Gettysburg Address, 81-84
    inauguration, first, 20-21, 91
    inauguration, second, 91, 93-96
    as lawyer, 15, 27, 29, 33, 36, 42, 46, 55
    and Lincoln-Douglas debates, 50-52

marriage, 31, 32-33
political career, 11, 15-18, 27, 28, 35-43, 48-55, 87-91
as president, 11, 18-21, 57-99
presidential elections, 11, 15-18, 54-55, 57, 87-91
and Reconstruction, 80-81, 85, 90, 91, 92-97
and slavery, 15, 26, 39-41, 43, 46-49, 52, 66, 69-70, 72, 75-76, 95
Lincoln, Edward Baker (son), 35, 45, 76
Lincoln, Mary Todd, 32-33, 35-36, 37-38, 45, 65, 76, 97, 98-99
Lincoln, Nancy Hanks (mother), 23, 25, 26
Lincoln, Robert Todd (son), 33
Lincoln, Sarah Bush Johnston (stepmother), 25-26
Lincoln, Thomas (father), 23, 25, 26, 27, 45
Lincoln, Thomas "Tad" (son), 45, 76, 96
Lincoln, William Wallace (son), 45, 65, 76, 82
Lincoln, Sarah (sister), 24
Logan, Stephen, 33

McClellan, George B., 62-65, 66, 69, 70, 89, 91

McDowell, Irvin, 62
Manifest Destiny, 12
Meade, George C., 79
Mexican War of 1846, 42, 43, 66
Missouri Compromise, 14

National Banking Act, 79
Native Americans, 27
New Salem, Illinois, 27, 28, 42

Panic of 1837, 30
Pickett, George E., 80

Reconstruction, 80-81, 85, 90, 91, 92-97
Republican party, 15, 49, 50, 51, 52, 54, 55, 63, 64, 70, 89
Roosevelt, Franklin D., 23

Scott, Dred, 14, 51, 52
Secession, 17-18, 46, 57, 60
Seward, William, 50, 52, 55
Sherman, William T., 85, 88, 91, 92
Shurz, Carl, 59
Slavery, 12-15, 26, 39-41, 43, 46-49, 51, 52, 66, 69-70, 72, 75-76, 91, 93, 95, 99
Slave trade, 12, 13, 14, 41, 47
Springfield, Illinois, 11,

18, 20, 28-30, 32, 36-37, 55
Stuart, John, 29, 33
Supreme Court, U.S., 14, 51

Taylor, Zachary, 43
Thanksgiving, 85
Thirteenth Amendment, 91, 99
Transcontinental railroad, 79
Trumball, Lyman, 49

Washington, George, 11, 26, 58
Webster, Daniel, 28, 42
Whig Party, 28, 29, 41, 42, 43, 49-50
Whitney, Eli, 12

PICTURE CREDITS

page
2: National Portrait Gallery, Washington D.C./Art Resource
10: The Lincoln Museum, Fort Wayne, IN#0-60
13: New York Public Library
15: Missouri Historical Society
16: Schomburg Center for Research in Black Culture, NYPL
19: Library of Congress, #62-11191
20: The Lincoln Museum, Fort Wayne, IN#0-54
22: The Lincoln Museum, Fort Wayne, IN#0-1
24: Illinois State Historical Library
25: The Abraham Lincoln Museum, Harrogate, TN
29: The Lincoln Museum, Fort Wayne, IN#603
30: Illinois State Historical Library
32: Library of Congress, #62-12458
34: The Lincoln Museum, Fort Wayne, IN#0-6
37: The Lincoln Museum, Fort Wayne, IN#0-38
38: Illinois State Historical Library
40: Library of Congress, #B8171
44: The Lincoln Museum, Fort Wayne, IN#0-36
46: Library of Congress, #61-1120
48: The Kansas State Historical Society, Topeka
50: Library of Congress, #62-29291
53: National Portrait Gallery, Smithsonian Institution/Art Resource, NY
56: Library of Congress, #62-5500
59: Library of Congress, #B8172-170
60: Army's Brady Collection
63: Library of Congress, #B8171
64: Illinois State Historical Library
67: Library of Congress, #B8171-560
68: National Portrait Gallery, Washington D.C./Art Resource, NY
71: (left)Library of Congress, #B8151-10067; (top)Library of Congress, #B8172-1625; (bottom) Library of Congress, #B8172-6385
74: National Portrait Gallery, Smithsonian Institution/Art Resource, NY
77: National Portrait Gallery, Smithsonian Institution/Art Resource, NY
78: The Lincoln Museum, Fort Wayne, IN#0-93
81: Library of Congress, #B8171-1228
82: Library of Congress, #B8184-7942
84: Library of Congress, #62-3117
86: Library of Congress, #62-13016
89: Library of Congress, #B8184-B-36
90: Library of Congress, #B8184-3611
93: Library of Congress, #B8184-7193
94: The Lincoln Museum, Fort Wayne, IN#4080
95: Library of Congress, #B8184-10701
98: photo © Judy L. Hasday
101: The Lincoln Museum, Fort Wayne, IN#99
104: Library of Congress, #B8171-7773

Thomas Bracken teaches American History at the City University of New York, and has taught at Mercy College. A former recipient of a grant from the Ford Foundation to conduct independent historical research, he created a CD-ROM to be used as a review guide in conjunction with college curriculums, and has published biographies of Theodore Roosevelt and William McKinley. Mr. Bracken lives in New Jersey.

James Scott Brady serves on the board of trustees with the Center to Prevent Handgun Violence and is the Vice Chairman of the Brain Injury Foundation. Mr. Brady served as Assistant to the President and White House Press Secretary under President Ronald Reagan. He was severely injured in an assassination attempt on the president, but remained the White House Press Secretary until the end of the administration. Since leaving the White House, Mr. Brady has lobbied for stronger gun laws. In November 1993, President Bill Clinton signed the Brady Bill, a national law requiring a waiting period on handgun purchases and a background check on buyers.